# WHIGS AND LIBERALS

# Whigs and Liberals

*Continuity and Change in English Political Thought*

THE CARLYLE LECTURES 1985

J. W. Burrow

CLARENDON PRESS · OXFORD

*This book has been printed digitally and produced in a standard design
in order to ensure its continuing availability*

# OXFORD
UNIVERSITY PRESS

Great Clarendon Street  Oxford OX2 6DP
Oxford University Press is a department of the University of Oxford
It furthers the University s objective of excellence in research  scholarship
and education by publishing worldwide in

Oxford  New York

Athens  Auckland  Bangkok  Bogotá  Buenos Aires  Cape Town
Chennai  Dar es Salaam  Delhi  Florence  Hong Kong  Istanbul  Karachi
Kolkata  Kuala Lumpur  Madrid  Melbourne  Mexico City  Mumbai
Nairobi  Paris  São Paulo  Singapore  Taipei  Tokyo  Toronto  Warsaw

with associated companies in  Berlin  Ibadan

Oxford is a registered trade mark of Oxford University Press
in the UK and certain other countries

Published in the United States
by Oxford University Press Inc  New York

© J  W  Burrow 1988

The moral rights of the author have been asserted
Database right Oxford University Press (maker)

Reprinted 2001

All rights reserved  No part of this publication may be reproduced
stored in a retrieval system  or transmitted  in any form or by any means
without the prior permission in writing of Oxford University Press
or as expressly permitted by law  or under terms agreed with the appropriate
reprographics rights organization  Enquiries concerning reproduction
outside the scope of the above should be sent to the Rights Department
Oxford University Press  at the address above

You must not circulate this book in any other binding or cover
and you must impose the same condition on any acquirer

ISBN 0-19-820139-7

For
Sir John Plumb
in gratitude

# Preface

THIS book has its origin in the Carlyle Lectures, delivered in the Oxford Hilary Term, 1985, and the first obligation to be acknowledged is to the endowment in memory of A. J. Carlyle which made it possible for me to spend the term in Oxford, and to the electors who honoured me by their choice. I am also deeply grateful to the Warden and Fellows of All Souls College not only for the splendid hospitality of their house but for their personal kindness, and to the friends in Oxford who made me welcome. I am, in addition, obliged to the University of Sussex for granting me the necessary leave.

The book derives its character from the circumstances of its origin. The Carlyle Lectures, devoted by the terms of the endowment to political theory, are intended to be of wide interest; had they been addressed to historians only I might have written mine rather differently In revising them I have both added to them and tried to prune them of what seemed too oratorical. In the latter I have not altogether succeeded. I tried, that is, to rewrite them as they might have appeared had I planned them as a book from the first, only to find that whatever vitality they possess came from the manner in which they were written, and that although I could make them duller I could not alter their essential character Hence they are presented more or less as they were delivered: as lectures. Each except the first and last is a kind of narrative, starting at roughly the same chronological point, but the book as a whole is an attempt not so much to write a sequential 'history of ideas' as to depict the shifting features of political culture seen from different angles. In the later lectures there are frequent reminiscences of earlier ones, as the subjects with which they deal are progressively seen as related. Whether these recapitulations are excessive is a matter of judgement, and mine may sometimes have erred, but they are the result of design, not negligence.

It may be helpful to say something more about the broad intention with which the lectures were written. One was to attempt a more coherent and general account than I have given hitherto of some closely related themes, in the work of nineteenth-century authors, which have interested me over a period of more than twenty years. Accordingly, the text of the lectures recalls in various places points I have made, sometimes more elaborately, in earlier published work. To talk of synthesis here would be a large overstatement; nevertheless, I have deliberately chosen sometimes to rework fragments in what I hope is a coherent way, in preference to the alternative possibility of a collection of reprinted essays and articles.

I must not exaggerate the suggestion of coherence; if it is implicit in earlier work, its presence is, for me, largely a retrospective discovery Yet I have found my occasional pillaging of earlier selves easy and even inevitable, testifying to a long-standing interest in the impact of historicist ways of thinking on European, and above all British, culture in the post-Romantic period. In particular I have been interested not so much in their tendency to issue in deterministic doctrines of historical inevitability as in the more or less tightly controlling context they offered to Romantic and Liberal—and I would also want to say Whig—conceptions of variety or diversity as essential to social and individual energy and vitality By the mid-nineteenth century this presumed connection had become, most famously but by no means exclusively in the writings of J. S. Mill, the foundation of liberal notions of progress, which had in turn become the touchstone of much else in moral, political, and cultural criticism.

The central idea here is one which, differently accented, has interested me at various times in Herbert Spencer, Wilhelm von Humboldt, Maitland, and Bagehot, and has made frequent reference to Burke inescapable. Although most distinctively associated with Romanticism, it can usefully be seen in relation to ideas long prominent, not always congruously, in European political and moral thinking: rights, civility, and the moral energy or public virtue which the eighteenth century opposed to luxury and servility In Britain, characteristically, the notion of variety as the condition of vitality became mingled, it is argued here, with the traditional Whig concern with the countervailing powers making up a complex or mixed sovereign, seen as the indispensable guardian of rights or of that independence which was the precondition of civic energy and virtue. The alarmed response of a number of English Liberals, towards the end of the nineteenth century, to the alien democratic sovereign which now confronted them with what seemed a terrifying simplicity akin to tyranny gives the story its obvious finale; attempts to accommodate Liberalism to democracy through devolved or less directly political forms of plurality provide the coda. The disillusionment of mid-Victorian Liberals, often marked by the political transition to Liberal Unionism, and the emergence of pluralist ideas as an important strand in early twentieth-century English political thought are both familiar themes. I have taken the latter as the subject of the final lecture both because of its appropriateness as a kind of Whiggism for the twentieth century and in the hope that our understanding of it is enhanced by placing it in this way I have tried elsewhere to trace the relations of Maitland's pluralism, in particular, to English Whig historiography I consider it again here, in a wider context.

But the attempt to reorder some of my own earlier thoughts has been very much secondary to the main intention of these lectures, which is to use the transformation (for it is no less) in recent years of the historiography of eighteenth-century political thought to provide new perspectives for looking at the period I myself know better, the nineteenth century This intention brings with it a characteristic and in a sense unavoidable difficulty, which should be confessed. It is the difficulty presented by a moving target. Eighteenth-century English political thinking was, as we have come to learn, itself immensely complex, and the study of it today is lively to the point of volatility But in practice to write about continuities entails assuming a certain stability in one's starting-point, which one knows to be artificial and which stands in naïve and implausible contrast to the fluidity and complexity of the subsequent stories one hopes to tell. That my own treatment of eighteenth-century themes should have something of this implausible simplicity is unavoidable as well as perhaps, in some places, culpable. But it has to be emphasized that I make no claim to add to our understanding of eighteenth-century political ideas as such. I have attempted only to present, selectively but I hope without actual travesty, what I have learnt from recent studies of that period, in order subsequently to use it for my own purposes, and tried not to put on my borrowed plumes too awkwardly or inappropriately, while fully acknowledging where they have been gathered. Nevertheless, my selection of them is necessarily made with an eye on the future, and for that reason, if for no other, it should not be taken as a general guide to the eighteenth-century notions on which it touches. In presenting, chiefly, the concept of politeness as the distinctively modern form of virtue, and the resulting confidence in the experience of social change as characteristic of an establishment Whiggism, it cannot attempt to do justice to the complexity with which that theme interacted with others in eighteenth-century political and moral discourse, or to the fact that current studies of eighteenth-century political thought produce not only usable conclusions but keen debate and continuing modifications. I have found them a stimulus as well as a starting-point, and I have tried to suggest what seem to me some of the main points of continuity, analogy, and difference in the nineteenth-century versions of Whiggism and Liberalism with which I deal, and which are admittedly far from fully comprehensive. Others will no doubt consider these questions, as some have already done, more fully and to better effect, as well as raising some not considered here at all.

One final word of explanation is called for by the title. To speak of a book whose leading figures include Hume, Smith, Burke, Jeffrey, and Mackintosh as concerned with 'English' political thought may seem unjustifiably annexationist. I must therefore say that 'English' political thought here means 'British', and Scots and Irishmen made a disproportionate contribution to it.

I am particularly grateful to Larry Siedentop, Quentin Skinner, John Thompson, and Patricia Williams for reading and criticizing the manuscript. They have done much to make me see its limitations and deficiencies; if I have not done all I should to repair them, the fault is entirely mine. I also owe a large debt to Mary Dunnington for her tireless kindness and patience in typing the manuscript. I am greatly indebted to the editorial staff at Oxford University Press for their helpfulness, patience, and care in preparing the book for the printer

I have left the greatest of my debts to the end. The amount I owe to Stefan Collini and Donald Winch is by no means adequately indicated by the citations of their works, numerous though these are, or by an acknowledgement of my gratitude to them for reading the manuscript and making many criticisms and suggestions. They have educated me by their conversation over many years, and though this book is very different in conception and organization I am sure I could not have written it as I have done but for the experience of collaborating with them in an earlier one, *That Noble Science of Politics*. It should be needless to say that they are in no way responsible for the present book's defects, but if it has virtues these are in large measure owed to them.

J.W.B.

# Contents

| | | |
|---|---|---|
| 1 | Whigs and Liberals | 1 |
| 2. | Polity and Society | 21 |
| 3 | The Sovereignty of Opinion | 50 |
| 4 | Autonomy and Self-realization: From Independence to Individuality | 77 |
| 5 | Balance and Diversity· From Roman Corruption to Chinese Stationariness | 101 |
| 6. | Subordinate Partialities: Sinister Interests and Corporate Rights | 125 |
| Index | | 155 |

# 1
# Whigs and Liberals

'MR CARLYLE has recently demonstrated the continuity of political thought from Cicero to Rousseau.'[1] This remark by J. N Figgis, in his classic lectures on the history of political thought, points to a daunting precedent. My own concern with continuity, in these lectures named in memory of A. J. Carlyle, is less extensive. Lord Acton identified the first Whig as St Thomas Aquinas. Macaulay, admitting that he used the word 'Whig' in no narrow sense, still went no further back for the first members of his 'great party' than the Elizabethan opponents of monopolies. Edward Freeman seems to have hankered to nominate Earl Godwin of Wessex. Dr Johnson, as we all know, said that the first Whig was the Devil. All these candidates are before my period.

That period extends roughly from the mid-eighteenth to the later nineteenth century, with excursions where appropriate on either side of these limits. But even in taking a period of rather over a hundred years, I skirt, if I do not run into, a typical danger for the historian of political thought. The amorphousness of his subject-matter, compared with that of the historian of institutions or of politics, is a constant temptation to reification, to the manufacture of spurious traditions out of superficial or accidental resemblances. The danger will be greater, obviously, the briefer the account, and the remedy Carlyle adopted, of producing six successive volumes of densely illustrated scholarship, calls for stamina few of us possess.[2] There may seem, too, a rather painful contrast between what I shall attempt and the most characteristic virtues of political

[1] J. N. Figgis, *Studies of Political Thought from Gerson to Grotius 1414–1625* (2nd edn., Cambridge University Press, 1916), 27
[2] Robert and A. J. Carlyle, *A History of Medieval Political Theory in the West*, 6 vols. (London, 1903–36). Figgis's reference was clearly to A. J. Carlyle. His brother Robert was recognized to have been the minor collaborator.

history as it is now practised. It is typically the chosen style of the modern political historian, compared with his Victorian Whig predecessors, to break down the categories, especially those of the political theorist; to identify the diversity of mores and interests, and the sometimes fortuitous or ironic conjunctions of these, in political movements or parties; and to attend to their regional and personal variations, their fluctuations from year to year and from issue to issue.

Compared with this cultivated sensitivity to the particular, the search for continuities advertised by my title, even the embarrassing if unavoidable and suitably qualified references to Whigg*ism* in which I shall sometimes indulge, may seem to indicate an old-fashioned, almost Macaulayan, search for a mythic Whig identity and its Liberal heir. I cannot, of course, guarantee that I shall not inadvertently produce a Whig history of Whiggism and Liberalism. I can only promise that if I do it will be inadvertent, and that I am aware not only of the perhaps avoidable dangers of naïve reification but also of the quite unavoidable prices to be paid in what I shall do. By taking as the subject of each of the subsequent lectures not an author, or an episode, or a period, or a debate, but a piece of political vocabulary, I forgo certain desirable kinds of particularity I shall be able to attend only perfunctorily to the individual temperaments and motives, and the political circumstances, which gave the uses of such language their urgency, and to the specific reservations by which they were often hedged. But for every strategy there is a price, and in this case (though not necessarily in others) I have thought it worth paying.

In the past, one obstacle to an understanding of intellectual continuities between Whigs and Liberals has been that philosophical model of liberal individualism which, by some rather drastic methods of recruitment and sometimes the elision of the word 'Whig' in favour of a prospective use of 'liberal', located the origins of liberalism in seventeenth-century theories of the state of nature and the social contract, and in doing so tacitly proclaimed an absence of concern with what eighteenth-century Whig ideas may have been when viewed in their own terms. As a narrative it thereupon generally lost interest in itself until the emergence of an elaborated utilitarianism in Bentham, and the advent of Political Economy It is a familiar part of the strategy of this account—the reclassification of seventeenth- and eighteenth-century principles in essentially nineteenth-century terms—that Locke and Smith, for example, must be rechristened 'liberals', while the same retrospective trick turns Burke into a 'conservative' The successive moments of the liberal tradition so constructed are a few fundamental texts: Hobbes and Locke; sometimes Hume—the *Treatise*, not the *Essays*—and Adam Smith; Bentham, Ricardo, and James Mill; J. S. Mill—at this point the tradition develops a certain amount of wobble—and Herbert Spencer. From these—in some cases in a highly selective reading—was constructed a political archetype, liberal individualism, a logically coherent body of epistemological, psychological, economic, and ethical doctrines, with a historical embodiment as 'the liberal tradition' Its essential components are individualism, rationalism, and utilitarianism. The ultimate units of its analytic scheme are autonomous individuals, rationally seeking the satisfaction of given wants. These wants are given by man's nature and by the accidents of mental association; they are not rationally ordered in any moral hierarchy of ends. Order is present in human society not in the realm of ends, where we are competitors for satisfactions which are both essentially private in their enjoyment and scarcely relative to the demand for them, but only in the rationality of our choice of means. Liberalism so defined is readily presented as the philosophical counterpart to *laissez-faire* Political Economy It makes the central political issue of liberal thought, and hence, by extension of nineteenth-century England, that of state intervention in economic life, which conveniently coincides with our own preoccupations with whether and how to run a mixed economy

Thanks to the work of historians of political thought over the past couple of decades, this model no longer offers convincing guidance to any large-scale interpretation of political theory in the seventeenth and eighteenth centuries, even if such an interpretation is still useful to those for whom history is more a matter of convenience than interest. But I am not sure that it does not, if only tacitly and by omission, still shape our sense of what constitutes the central line, as it were, of nineteenth-century English political thought. It would not be surprising if it did; it would certainly have more historical justification than its application to earlier centuries. It is at least reassuring that, after the early decades of the nineteenth century, liberals were self-proclaimed as such, without the need for anachronistic rebaptism. We should not make too much of this—the divergences among liberals were more than nuances—but it is certainly true, as proponents of the model would always have acknowledged, that its most complete exemplars are nineteenth-century ones like James Mill or Herbert Spencer The price we pay for making nineteenth-century liberalism the culmination of a story focused exclusively in this way, however, is the impoverishment of our sense of possible connections between nineteenth-century liberal thinking and the richly heterogeneous varieties of eighteenth-century Whiggism. The omission of these was, as for example in the vital case of Adam Smith, the precondition of seeing the history of eighteenth-century social and political thought primarily or exclusively in terms of its supposed logical fulfilment in *laissez-faire* individualism.

In fact, of course, the claims of the liberal-individualist model to provide an interpretation of intellectual history have always been characterized by a certain ambiguity When Sheldon Wolin, for example, in his *Politics and Vision* (a good example because clearly more concretely historical in its intention than many—it is only an obligation to do history if history is what you claim to be doing), spoke of 'liberal man',[3] he offered an ideal-type whose intended scope and purchase in the history of thought were not readily apparent. It seemed that we were to think of the story of liberalism told there as a broadly cultural and political rather than a restrictedly philosophical one, yet the empirical responsibilities assumed were not altogether clear. In a statement like 'the Hobbesian model of society was implicitly adopted by the liberalism of the next two centuries as its own',[4] some kind of historical claim certainly seems to be made. Yet the use of 'implicitly'—a well-known device for foisting a *reductio ad absurdum*—and the cavalier methods,

---

[3] Sheldon Wolin, *Politics and Vision: Continuity and Innovation in Western Political Thought* (Boston, 1960), 324.
[4] Ibid. 282. Wolin makes the point that the model was assumed by *critics* of liberalism like de Maistre.

historically speaking, by which the ranks of liberalism are recruited or limited at will make it seem that what is asserted in this way of talking may be more like a covert tautology, an indication of the kind of statement to be counted in this idiom as a liberal utterance. If that is so then we shall merely make ourselves look foolish by attempting to show, as would not be difficult, the extreme rarity with which a Hobbesian model of society was explicitly adopted in the English political discourse of the eighteenth and nineteenth centuries, or even the absence of anything much like a Hobbesian conception of man in most of those whom contemporaries would have identified as Liberal. Perhaps there were just not many liberals in this sense. In fact the assertion can be made at all plausible only by assuming the virtually complete subsumption of the political into the economic. This is, indeed, the point of the exercise, but the method of establishing it contains more than a suggestion of circularity· 'to the liberals action meant first and foremost economic action.'[5]

Such logical model-building is obviously useful for the purpose of philosophical critique. It emphasizes precision and logical consistency, and tends to treat anything that does not fit as residues or mere incoherence. In this it is very like Utilitarianism and very unlike Whiggism, and its historical attention tends to be focused accordingly As Hume said, it is difficult to find the words to express the mean between extremes.[6] But as a way of rendering something more like the vigour and activity of past intellectual life, with its complex ways of accommodating, combining, and manipulating, under various kinds of pressure, the rival theoretical languages which' a rich political culture contains, it is severely limited and may even be misleading. It is often more helpful, in writing the history of political thought, to think of political theories as vocabularies we inhabit, with their various claims, opportunities, and constraints, than as doctrines to which we subscribe. That history is messy is a truth we need not lose hold of because the history we choose to write is the history of political thought, and if we do not retain it, we shall

[5] Ibid. 300.
[6] David Hume, *Essays Moral, Political and Literary*, eds. T H. Green and T H. Grose, 2 vols. (London, 1875), 1. 121.

have to be content with something like a Hegelian procession of abstract Ideas and their supposed historical embodiments. Because of their rigorous abstraction from the ways groups of people actually conducted their arguments, these abstractions in turn naturally generate puzzles about their relation to another abstraction, 'social reality' [7]

Here, however, I shall not be concerned with the construction of philosophical systems in the past, or the retrospective imposition of schematic abstractions upon it. Nor, on the other hand, shall I generally be dealing with the rhetorical tactics of the immediate pursuit of policy or party advantage. What I consider here under the name of 'political thought' lies for the most part in the space between them. It is neither highly abstract and tightly coherent nor immediately effective, and so is apt to be slighted by political philosophers and ideologues as well as by political historians. But it is not therefore negligible: it is the reflective articulation of the educated classes' political culture. To speak of it in terms of Whiggism and Liberalism is to encompass, in the period we are considering, not the whole of it, but a substantial part. My own concern with it here will be more partial again, excluding Benthamism and Political Economy I shall not touch, either, on that politically immensely important strain of moralistic liberalism grounded above all in the culture of Dissent. To trace its origins in the eighteenth century would almost certainly take us back to the radical Lockianism of the age of the American Revolution, and this I shall not attempt. Such selectivity is harmless provided it is fully acknowledged, and it can also be usefully corrective.

Even if we confine ourselves more strictly to theory, however, it has become implausible to simplify the history of political ideas in Britain, from the later seventeenth century, into the emergence of liberal individualism. The chief heroes of the putative 'tradition', Locke and Adam Smith, have

---

[7] Hegel and Marx continue to be bound together by mutual need, the one for an *explanans*, the other for an *explanandum*, produced by the former's conflation of philosophy and history *Ce n'est que le premier pas qui coûte*. The reflections on political language above follow the lines of J. G. A. Pocock's 'Languages and their Implications: The Transformation of the Study of Political Thought', in his *Politics, Language and Time* (London, 1972).

proved, when looked at closely, decidedly recalcitrant to their recruitment in this fashion.⁸ Even Burke seems only very partially assimilable to his old role as reactionary organicist critic (so much so that attempts have been made, somewhat less plausibly, to recruit him to the liberal-individualist story not as an opponent but as a disguised exponent of central features of the creed).⁹ But it is not only a matter of a more historically sophisticated exegesis of the great figures. Our whole picture of the world of eighteenth-century political discourse has been immensely enlarged and complicated.¹⁰ Instead of a story from which, in its sparer and more 'philosophical' versions, even the word 'Whig' tended to disappear, we are required to distinguish True or Real Whigs, Court Whigs, Establishment or Regime Whigs, Ciceronian and Catonic Whigs,¹¹ sceptical, scientific, and vulgar Whigs, Country Whigs, radical Whigs, and two distinct species of New and Old Whigs, and there are no doubt other potentially useful distinctions (some of those listed are, admittedly, overlapping or even identical categories).¹² Yet this profusion has only fairly recently begun to fertilize the study of even the early

⁸ John Dunn, *The Political Thought of John Locke: An Historical Account of the Argument of the 'Two Treatises of Government'* (Cambridge University Press, 1969); Donald Winch, *Adam Smith's Politics: An Essay in Historiographic Revision* (Cambridge University Press, 1978).
⁹ C. B. Macpherson, *Burke* (Oxford University Press, 1981); Isaac Kramnick, *The Rage of Edmund Burke* (New York, 1977). For a critical discussion see Donald Winch, 'The Burke-Smith Problem and late Eighteenth-century Political and Economic Thought', *Historical Journal*, 28/1 (1985), 231–47
¹⁰ For a judgement of the general (adverse) implications of recent historiography for the interpretation of 18th-cent. political thought as essentially the story of the emergence of liberal (or 'bourgeois') individualism, see J. G. A. Pocock, *Virtue, Commerce and History: Essays on Political Thought and History Chiefly in the Eighteenth Century* (Cambridge University Press, 1985), 57, 60–1, 71, 111, 241–2.
¹¹ Reed Browning, *Political and Constitutional Ideas of the Court Whigs* (London, 1982), 3–8, and esp. ch. VIII.
¹² No account of the significance of these distinctions can possibly be attempted here. For general surveys of 18th-cent. political ideas see H. T Dickinson, *Liberty and Property: Political Ideology in Eighteenth-century Britain* (London, 1977), and, most recently, the compressed but characteristically suggestive remarks by J. G. A. Pocock, *Virtue, Commerce and History*, Part III, 'The Varieties of Whiggism from Exclusion to Reform: A History of Ideology and Discourse', Istvan Hont and Michael Ignatieff (eds.), *Wealth and Virtue: The Shaping of Political Economy in the Scottish Enlightenment* (Cambridge University Press, 1983), is also now a rich source of studies on the Scottish Enlightenment and its interaction with other 18th-cent. intellectual traditions.

part of the nineteenth century,[13] nor is it yet clear when, why, and how some of the categories become inappropriate in our mapping of nineteenth-century political thought.

One way we can approach such questions is to look at a point at which the political ideas of the eighteenth century had come to seem of purely 'historical' interest (at most) and to see how selective and restricted that interest appears to be. Of course, conscious interest of this kind is not the whole story; people may be influenced by more subterranean intellectual traditions than they are aware of. But it is a start, and with this in mind we may look at an early attempt consciously to treat the ideas of eighteenth-century England historically· Leslie Stephen's *English Thought in the Eighteenth Century*, first published in 1876, particularly the chapter on political thought. Stephen was deeply interested at the time in social and moral philosophy But despite that, or rather because of it, his attitude to eighteenth-century political thought is notably dismissive: 'In the quieter hours of the eighteenth century Englishmen rather played with political theories than seriously discussed them.'[14] The ordinary political discourse of the time consisted of 'generalities about liberty, corruption and luxury' [15] It was also essentially unoriginal. Locke's exposition of the principles of 1688 became the political bible of the eighteenth century;[16] Locke himself is presented as a thwarted utilitarian, unfortunately entangled in the contract metaphor—'this vexatious figment', as Stephen calls it.[17] Bolingbroke's 'Patriot King' is simply an absurdity [18] Hume was a cynical conservative,

---

[13] Among noteworthy recent studies apart from Pocock, *Virtue*, which enhance our understanding of the years between 1789 and 1832 and to which I am indebted are J. E. Cookson, *The Friends of Peace: Anti-war Liberalism in England, 1793-1815* (Cambridge University Press, 1982); Biancamaria Fontana, *Rethinking the Politics of Commercial Society: The Edinburgh Review 1802-1832* (Cambridge University Press, 1985); Leslie Mitchell, *Holland House* (London, 1980); William Thomas, *The Philosophic Radicals* (Oxford University Press, 1979); and essays I-III (by Donald Winch) in Stefan Collini, Donald Winch, and John Burrow, *That Noble Science of Politics: A Study of Nineteenth-century Intellectual History* (Cambridge University Press, 1983). In addition, what is said above is obviously not intended to deny that there has been exploration of the roots of early 19th-cent. Radicalism in the radical Whig doctrines of the later 18th-cent., notably in E. P Thompson, *The Making of the English Working-Class* (London, 1963), esp. chs. 3, 13, 15, 16.

[14] Leslie Stephen, *English Thought in the Eighteenth Century* (1876), 2 vols. (London, 1962), ii. 111.

[15] Ibid.   [16] Ibid. 114.   [17] Ibid. 118.   [18] Ibid. 148.

Ferguson a 'facile and dextrous declaimer';[19] Millar is not mentioned at all. Hume 'takes a statical view of history and thus unconsciously ignores all theories of evolution' (We may well ponder 'unconsciously ignores' )[20] Despite his ostensible interest in national character, men for him 'are but the abstract man—the metaphysical entity, alike in all times, places and conditions'[21] The only hero of the story, ushering in modernity and making the break between the eighteenth and nineteenth centuries, is Burke. Bentham, incidentally, whom one might have expected to figure here also, was dealt with in the chapter on ethics, and essentially reserved for Stephen's later three-volume study of the Utilitarians. But Burke is the eighteenth-century theorist who uniquely understands 'the conception of a nation as a living organism of complex structure and historical continuity', and who understands that a constitution is, as he said, 'a vestment which accommodates itself to the body'[22] The effect, given Stephen's account of Burke's contemporaries and predecessors, is virtually to detach him from his century and his intellectual and political milieu, in the cause of converting him into a forerunner of late nineteenth-century social evolutionism.

We should, of course, resist the temptation to condescend to our predecessors for condescending to theirs. It is not at all surprising that almost everything in Stephen's account now seems to need revision: in selection, omission, emphasis, and interpretation. But as a view from the 1870s it is highly relevant to our general theme. It is easy enough to see the various influences which shaped Stephen's account. He wrote as a man preoccupied with the question of scientifically grounded social ethics and with the hope that social evolutionism might provide this—a preoccupation which a little later produced his massive book *The Science of Ethics*. For him, social evolutionism was the necessary corrective to, but also in some sense the consummation of, the utilitarian enterprise; he wrote therefore as one for whom the central story of English political thought was the emergence of liberal utilitarianism and its subsequent

---

[19] Ibid. 182.     [20] Ibid. 154.
[21] Ibid. 155. Also, typical of the 1870s is Stephen's reference to neglect of 'race', ibid. 154–7
[22] Ibid. 195, 193.

modification by the organic metaphor.²³ His cast of mind and interests were in any case by this time philosophical rather than directly political or historical. To Stephen it was a reproach, not a compliment, when he said that, in the eighteenth century, political philosophy 'is generally embedded in discussion of concrete facts' ²⁴

But there are other features of interest in Stephen's account which emerge if we compare him with some of his nineteenth-century predecessors as commentators on the eighteenth century There is a strain of mid-Victorian moral earnestness and strenuousness in his distaste for eighteenth-century minds. He writes from a self-consciously rugged and would-be rigorous conception of moral and intellectual merit, in which 'manliness', 'truth', 'sincerity', and 'science' are related terms, and he predictably found most of the eighteenth century wanting. Thus, Shaftesbury was an aesthete with no understanding of the real world, Bishop Butler a victim of metaphysical complacency, Hume, as we have seen, a cynic.²⁵ All, we are made to feel, let themselves off too easily It is with an air of unmistakable moral as well as intellectual relief that Stephen turns to Burke, to the 'nobility of his moral nature', and a political culture hospitable to the heartfelt sublime.²⁶ Stephen belonged to a generation which had Romanticism and Evangelicalism as part of its heritage, and science and evolution as its newly acquired creed, and which grew to political maturity in the 1860s; he was one of the contributors to the democratic manifesto of the University Liberals in 1867, *Essays on Reform*.²⁷ To that generation of young Liberals, Whiggism with its eighteenth-century affinities was not exactly a scorned opponent, as for the Philosophical Radicals earlier, but a clog on energy and enthusiasm: tepid, sceptical, weak-nerved, a senior partner whose day was done and whose continuing presence was an anachronistic encumbrance. The period of Stephen's intellectual and political coming of age surely

---

²³ See e.g. Leslie Stephen, *The English Utilitarians*, 3 vols. (London, 1900), iii. 375.
²⁴ *English Thought in the Eighteenth Century*, ii. 111.
²⁵ Ibid. 27, 66–7, 157                                                                                    ²⁶ Ibid. 188.
²⁷ On this group of young Liberals see Christopher Harvie, *The Lights of Liberalism: University Liberals and the Challenge of Democracy, 1860–1886* (London, 1976). I am substantially indebted to this useful and stimulating book.

conditioned his attitude to eighteenth-century political thought.²⁸ If Stephen's case is in any way typical, and I suggest it is, then the democratic, intellectual, young liberalism of the fifties and sixties represents a significant shift in political attitudes, and with it—and this is my point—a change in relation to the eighteenth century, a kind of disconnection which had not been there earlier In a Whig of an earlier generation, with his political baptism in the twenties and thirties—and it is inevitable to take Macaulay—this had not been so. Macaulay, sponsored on his entry into public life by the *Edinburgh Review* and Holland House, was not merely a student of, but manifestly a participant in, the political culture of the eighteenth century Through Holland House he was privy to the Foxite tradition enshrined there. If his own Whiggism was very differently accented, it was largely because he was—in a way no Liberal of the second half of the century that I can think of was—so aware of, and inherited, the central ideas of the Scottish Enlightenment.²⁹ Of Macaulay could almost be said, by a slight stretching of the hyperbole, what he said of Lord Holland, that while he lived 'all the great statesmen and orators of the last generation were living too' ³⁰ Even his pejorative references to standard components of eighteenth-century English political thought have an intimacy and casualness which it is hard to imagine in Stephen: Macaulay's contempt for the Machiavellian, Country Party and classical-republican, rhetoric of patriotic virtue, for example.³¹

Let us take another example, an intermediate figure between Macaulay and Stephen—intermediate in age and also in political culture: a liberal by conventional designation rather than a Whig, but certainly a more conservative one than

---

²⁸ Thus, for example, religious tests were a matter of acute interest, and to this may be due the fact that in his account of 18th-cent. political theories we get quite a full, if predictably weary, account of the Bangorian controversy The relief from the general present-mindedness of this chapter is only apparent: *English Thought in the Eighteenth Century*, ii. 129-41.

²⁹ John Clive, *Thomas Babington Macaulay: The Shaping of the Historian* (New York, 1973), 105-7; J. W Burrow, *A Liberal Descent: Victorian Historians and the English Past* (Cambridge University Press, 1981), 41-6.

³⁰ G. O. Trevelyan, *The Life and Letters of Lord Macaulay* (Popular Edn., London, 1899), 394-5.     ³¹ Burrow, *Liberal Descent*, pp. 55-9

Stephen, namely Bagehot.[32] Bagehot's political attitudes have sometimes been regarded as puzzling or unclassifiable, but a good deal of the puzzlement would perhaps evaporate if generation or social position had allowed us to call him a Whig. Bagehot, in some ways at least, seems a supporting case for Lord John Russell's retort to the Duke of Newcastle, when the latter suggested the abandonment of the old name, that 'Whig' expresses in one syllable what 'conservative liberal' says in seven.[33] Bagehot did not know the eighteenth century as Macaulay did, but the period from the 1770s onwards I think he did know with a good deal of intimacy It was knowledge, for example, which allowed an appreciation of Adam Smith that included far more than the *laissez-faire* godfather or straw man of nineteenth- and twentieth-century polemic.[34] On the franchise issue, in the 1860s, Bagehot reproduced all the old Whig arguments for representation by interests rather than numbers, and even criticized the provisions of the First Reform Act from this point of view [35] In constitutional matters he sometimes reads like a pupil of Jeffrey and Mackintosh.[36] He and Stephen, as it happens, both wrote essays on the Edinburgh Reviewers.[37] Bagehot's approval is qualified, but he is predictably warmer and more at ease than Stephen.[38] Threads of unselfconscious connection, still plainly visible in Macaulay, and drawn, understandably, a little thinner in Bagehot, in Stephen have snapped, and the latter will move on to reconstruct his own kind of intellectual heritage in his history of the English Utilitarians.

The claim that the 1860s make a kind of watershed in this

---

[32] Stephen, in his essay on Bagehot, found him, like Hume, a cynic, but clearly found his cynicism refreshing: Leslie Stephen, *Studies of a Biographer*, 4 vols. (London, 1907), iii. 144-75.
[33] Donald Southgate, *The Passing of the Whigs 1832-1886* (London, 1962), 237
[34] See 'Adam Smith as a Person', in *The Collected Works of Walter Bagehot*, ed. Norman St John-Stevas, 15 vols. (London, 1965-86), iii. 84-112.
[35] See *Works*, vi. 187-236. Cf. 'Lord Althorp and the Reform Act of 1832', iii. 200-32.
[36] On Jeffrey as precursor of Bagehot's version of the constitution see M. J. C. Vile, *Constitutionalism and the Separation of Powers* (Oxford University Press, 1967), 216.
[37] Bagehot, *Works*, i. 308-42; Stephen, *Hours in a Library*, 4 vols. (London, 1907), iii. 88-127
[38] Collini, Winch, and Burrow, *That Noble Science*, essay v, pp. 165-9

respect needs some qualifications which are not easy to put precisely. It was the democratic and republican enthusiasms[39] of Stephen's generation of young radical liberals, in the fifties and sixties, which cut them off from the more cautious Whiggism of Macaulay and Bagehot, which by that time formed the chief line of unbroken connection back to the eighteenth century. Yet the subsequent reaction, the disillusionment with democracy and fears for the future of liberalism, so prevalent among liberal intellectuals in the last three decades of the century, often takes forms which seem like a kind of nostalgic Whiggishness, and even an idealization of aspects of the eighteenth century. But it was idealization from a distance, a conscious regret rather than Macaulay's unselfconscious assumption of intimacy.

Sir Henry Maine, for example, in his onslaught on democracy in *Popular Government* (1885), devoted one of his four essays to praise of the checks and balances of the American constitution, as an intelligent adaptation, by the founding fathers, of English eighteenth-century constitutionalism to a democratic society. Faced in the 1880s by a unified Parliamentary sovereign, elected on a democratic franchise, the revival of the ideal of 'balance' through a formal separation of powers could seem an attractive proposition. W. E. H. Lecky also, in *Democracy and Liberty* (1896), presented a sympathetic picture of the unreformed English constitution, and celebrated the constitutional arrangements established in 1832 as virtually ideal. Yet Lecky, like Stephen, really seems another example of the fracture in the unselfconscious transmission of Whig political ideas. It is a disjunction all the more marked because he, like Stephen, was a leading authority—indeed, as far as politics and general history was concerned, for his contemporaries *the* leading authority—on the eighteenth century.

Lecky himself, as a latitudinarian Irish Protestant and a conservative Liberal, found nostalgic inspiration in the gentry-dominated, unsectarian Irish nationalism of Grattan's day, as well as constantly resorting wistfully to the notion of a constitutional balance of powers in ways which make it

[39] Harvie, *Lights of Liberalism*, passim.

appropriate to speak of him as a Whig *après la lettre*. Yet in his massive *History of England in the Eighteenth Century* (1878–90) he shows minimal recognition of the principled, argumentative dimension of eighteenth-century politics.[40] This is the more noteworthy in that it clearly did not come from any hostility to intellectual history as such. The author of *The Rise of Rationalism* (1865) and *The History of European Morals* (1869) was no proto-Namierite. Yet for all his fuller knowledge of eighteenth-century political life, he, like his contemporaries, was content to let Burke represent the pinnacle of eighteenth-century political reflection and care little about the foothills.

A symptom of a kind of revived Whiggism was in fact much attention to and echoing of Burke: in Leslie Stephen, Maine, Acton, Lecky, Freeman, Bryce, and John Morley, who wrote not one book about him but two. Of course Burke and Whiggism are protean enough to mean many things. When Acton said that behind Bryce's *American Commonwealth* there was 'a bewildered Whig', it was a palpable hit.[41] But when Figgis hailed Acton himself as the incarnation of 'the spirit of Whiggism', and Morley spoke of Maine as 'the most eminent English member of the Burkian School',[42] we are inclined to murmur reservations on behalf of the former's imperious Christian moralism and the latter's utilitarian *laissez-faire* individualism. Burke was made acceptable to Victorian minds by Christian earnestness and a Romantic organicism which could readily sound proto-Darwinian and hence modern. This was very much, as we have seen, Stephen's view Yet, seen in this way, Burke became, as we also saw, not a line of communication back to the eighteenth-century Whiggism, but a way of ignoring it, by treating him either in isolation from his period or as a summation of everything that might still be worth knowing about eighteenth-century political thought.

---

[40] I am indebted for a better understanding of Lecky to a recent comprehensive study of his political thought: Yvonne Dineen, 'The Problem of Political Stability in a Democratic Age: The Ideas of W E. H. Lecky' (University of Wales Ph.D. thesis, Swansea, 1986). I am grateful for the author's permission to make use of it.
[41] Quoted by Collini, in Collini, Winch, and Burrow, *That Noble Science*, p. 242.
[42] Introduction to Lord Acton, *The History of Freedom and Other Essays* (London, 1909), p. xxx; John Morley, *Notes on Politics and History* (2nd edn., London, 1914), 27

The cult of Burke was at least in part a case of the selectivity of ignorance or distaste. The unselfconscious transmission of a political culture is finally replaced by the cultivated recollection of a few exemplary great figures; not the preservation of a tradition, though it may be called that, but naïve intellectual history

Of course, the most startling of all examples of combined ignorance and distaste applied to the eighteenth century occurs in an earlier generation, with J. S. Mill, from whom, through his *Autobiography*, several generations have been apt to take their intellectual history of the first half of the nineteenth century For him the crucial conflict between a priori/deductive and empirical/historically grounded political theory was 'the fight between the nineteenth century and the eighteenth' [43] It is ironic that this makes Macaulay, in his controversy with Mill's father, the nineteenth-century figure, and James Mill the eighteenth-century one. Not because this antithesis needs reversing, but because historically the whole way of putting it is misleading,[44] derived, surely, not from Mill's knowledge of the eighteenth century but from his knowledge of Comte. For what is most striking of all, in his own account of his intellectual life, is that J. S. Mill should present as discoveries of the 1820s and 1830s, borrowed from France and Germany, notions of historical relativism and the historical determination of politics which would have seemed commonplace in the Edinburgh of Dugald Stewart and John Millar when his father was being educated there.[45]

But J. S. Mill is perhaps a special case, insulated from Whiggism by inherited hostility. In suggesting a sharp disconnection from eighteenth-century political thought in the mid-Victorian years, related to the decline of Whiggism, we must be careful not to exaggerate. The transmission of a political culture may be a subtler and more continuous matter than conscious awareness of it; what was broken, or at least drastically abridged, may sometimes have been rather more

---

[43] J. S. Mill, *Autobiography*, ed. J. Stillinger (Oxford University Press, 1971), 98.
[44] Winch, 'The Cause of Good Government', in Collini, Winch, and Burrow, *That Noble Science*, pp. 110 ff., shows how both were rooted in the ideas of the Scottish Enlightenment.
[45] Winch, 'The System of the North: Dugald Stewart and his Pupils', ibid. 23-63.

at the level of conscious knowledge and sympathy than conceptual transmission. Stephen saw this, I think, though he put it in his own way, in his essay on Macaulay—an essay in which, incidentally, while he predictably found Macaulay's scepticism in political theory and philosophy a form of philistinism, he nevertheless approved of his robustness, his 'hearty admiration for sheer manliness' Macaulay, he wrote,

must be interesting as long as the type which he so fully represents continues to exist. Whig has become an old-fashioned phrase, and is repudiated by modern Liberals and Radicals   The decay of the old name implies a remarkable political change; but I doubt whether it implies more than a very superficial change in the national character. New classes and new ideas have come upon the stage; but they have a curious family likeness to the old. The Whiggism whose peculiarities Macaulay reflected so faithfully represents some of the most deeply seated tendencies of the national character.[46]

Stephen, in the idiom of his period, spoke of 'national character' where I have spoken of the continuities of a political culture. These are seen most clearly perhaps in the accepted empirical generalizations about politics, infused, of course, with moral and political hope or anxiety, which thinkers of various creeds tended to assume, and which in turn helped to shape their more directly prescriptive doctrines. The reflections on political virtue and its conditions, on the enervation of public spirit, stasis, and the decline of states, that we meet in Mill's *Representative Government* would have raised no eyebrows in the eighteenth century; even the diction is not very dissimilar. Again, when Mill in *On Liberty* added something to the stock of ideas in contemporary political debate by his exaltation of variety, the specific line of connection to the eighteenth century is an extended loop, through Wilhelm von Humboldt to Shaftesbury [47] But more to the point is that, in stressing the value of variety, Mill unconsciously, in a post-Romantic vocabulary, and, as was usual with him, prompted by an immediate influence from the Continent, rejoined a pre-existing and powerful strain of English political thinking deeply rooted

[46] Stephen, *Hours in a Library*, iii. 269–70.
[47] The third Earl, of course, not Dryden's Achitophel: Wilhelm von Humboldt, *The Limits of State Action*, ed. and trans. J. W Burrow (Cambridge University Press, 1969), pp. xv, xxxii.

in eighteenth-century Whiggism, which the utilitarian insistence on the sovereignty of numbers had partially severed. One does not readily associate Mill, for example, with Burke, but just as the chief inspiration of Mill's *Representative Government* was Thomas Hare's plan for proportional representation, so the presiding genius of Hare's book, as his frequent references make clear, was Burke.[48]

So the question of unconscious or conscious connection is often a complicated one in the mid-nineteenth century If we can now see more clearly what questions to ask, if not their answers, our debt is to recent studies of eighteenth-century political thought. Only a quarter of a century ago or less, the standard historical version of eighteenth-century political thinking was not, I think, very different from the one we found in Stephen. Burke and Bentham, cherished, for different reasons, by political philosophers and historians, seemed to exhaust what was worth remembering, and both tended to be treated as early nineteenth-century figures. For historians concerned directly with the political life of the eighteenth century, Sir Lewis Namier's frown paralysed interest in political thought perhaps more peremptorily than in any other period. Our rediscovery of the complex patterns of eighteenth-century political theorizing belongs to the last twenty-five years. Thanks to it, we now know much more of the neo-classical, humanist, Machiavellian strain in eighteenth-century constitutionalism, and of its influence, both on Country Party ideas and on those of the American Revolution. The social and political theories of the Scottish Enlightenment too are far better, if not by any means fully, understood; in particular their attempts to come to terms with the civic-humanist antithesis between political liberty and the development of civilization, through a new conception of the development of civil society, replacing Machiavelli, as it were, by a more developed, historicized version of Montesquieu.[49] Our awareness of all this is quite recent, and it has been acquired by a deliberate scholarly determination to see the basic assumptions of

---

[48] Thomas Hare, *A Treatise on the Election of Representatives* (London, 1859), 2, 7, 21-2, 48-50, 56, etc.

[49] e.g. Donald Winch, *Adam Smith's Politics*; Hont and Ignatieff, *Wealth and Virtue*, passim.

eighteenth-century political argument as it was for the participants, rather than to look in it for anticipations of nineteenth- and twentieth-century concerns. And the possibility, to which I want to draw attention, now suggests itself, of attempting, as it were, to reverse the process—to look at nineteenth-century political thought, as far as may prove appropriate, in terms suggested by its eighteenth-century antecedents.

The work, I suppose, which more than any other has shaped, and perhaps continues to shape, our ways of perceiving nineteenth-century English political thought is now over eighty years old. Halévy's *The Growth of Philosophic Radicalism* is surely a great book; remarkable in its own time as a comprehensive synthesis of a crucial segment of English intellectual history; impressive still. I have no specific challenge to it in mind; my point is not its possible defects but its imposing merits, and I wonder if we have not a little suffered as well as learnt from its eminence, and from the predominance in our understanding of English nineteenth-century political thought of the liberal-individualist model, to which Halévy's work, it seems to me, is still the most impressive single historical contribution. Of course, I do not mean that nothing has been learnt. Thanks to the efforts of a number of scholars we know much more about Bentham and about Philosophic Radicalism itself. We also know more about popular radicalism, about the influence of Coleridge and Thomas Arnold, about Social Darwinism, about the intellectual liberalism of the 1860s and the New Liberalism of the last years of the century, infused by the philosophical Idealism of T H. Green and touched by what, to contemporaries at least, was 'socialism' But most of these belong to the middle and latter decades of the century; in the earlier ones, Philosophic Radicalism still tends to dominate our perceptions, and of course in any general account it must always play a major role, and my omission of it here is defensible only because I make no such claim to comprehensiveness.

But in making it central we necessarily push other ideas and traditions to the periphery In doing so, for example, we make nineteenth-century English social and political ideas more peculiar perhaps, in the context of European liberalism with its historicist and constitutionalist enthusiasms, than a more Whiggish perspective would do.[50] When Macaulay abused James Mill in the *Edinburgh Review* as a medieval schoolman, 'an Aristotelian of the fifteenth-century, born out of due season',[51] we may feel he chose, misled by his own preoccupation with Bacon, the wrong analogy· the true affinity was with Bacon's protégé Thomas Hobbes, and it was one the Utilitarians sometimes acknowledged. But we should, I think, try to understand Macaulay's exasperation, his quite genuine sense that the Utilitarians were not just, as he rightly called them, a sect, but also an anachronism, an anomaly in the development of an increasingly empirical, historically and comparatively grounded, but thoughtful and comprehensive political culture, whose highest articulation was the 'noble science of politics' Seen in this way, Utilitarianism is bound to seem something of a hiatus, an odd resurgence of a mode of political reasoning akin to seventeenth-century rationalism. And there are, after all, features of English liberal thought later in the century which give plausibility to the suggestion that strict, deductive utilitarian political theory of the kind exemplified in James Mill's *Essay on Government* should be seen as a kind of interruption. The English liberal enthusiasm for Tocqueville, for example, from the 1830s to the 1860s, introduced themes far more congruent with an eighteenth-century Whig heritage than with deductive utilitarianism.

Of course, Philosophic Radicalism remains a massively important fact in the intellectual history of nineteenth-century England, and it would be odd to call anything so diffusely influential an aberration, particularly when one follows the connection with Political Economy Yet there can sometimes be benefits in shifting our point of vantage, and looking in this case at the history of English political thought through the eyes of Macaulay rather than J. S. Mill or Leslie Stephen, in a way

---

[50] For this reason an important stimulus in defining the purpose of the lectures has been a fruitful disagreement with part of the argument of Larry Siedentop, 'Two Liberal Traditions', in Alan Ryan (ed.), *The Idea of Freedom: Essays in Honour of Isaiah Berlin* (Oxford University Press, 1979), 153–75.

[51] T B. Macaulay, 'Mill's Essay on Government' (1829), in Jack Lively and John Rees, *Utilitarian Logic and Politics: James Mill's 'Essay on Government' and Macaulay's Critique and the Ensuing Debate* (Oxford University Press, 1978), 101.

which makes continuity with eighteenth-century Whiggism seem the natural assumption to make, and which refuses to confine the eighteenth-century heritage to utilitarian ethics, association psychology, and a much-narrowed version of Political Economy

In the next lecture I begin by looking at what seems to me, more than any other, the controlling context, in various mutations, of eighteenth- and nineteenth-century political thought, the notion of the development of civil society, 'civilization', or what the nineteenth century came increasingly to call simply 'progress' The exploration of the vicissitudes of that concept, and of its assumed implications for politics, which to Hume and Smith were an important discovery, to Macaulay a platitude, and to J. S. Mill a recent revelation from Paris, was, far more than a rationalist individualism, the central programme of nineteenth-century political thought. In its broadest terms it was an inheritance from the eighteenth century Having established this as a context, I propose to go on in subsequent lectures to consider familiar and crucial elements in nineteenth-century liberalism, and to try to see how far they too can usefully be seen as mutations of eighteenth-century concepts: the importance assigned, with an increasing anxiety, to 'public opinion', the value attached to 'individuality' and to manifestations of 'diversity'

# 2
# Polity and Society

M. de Tocqueville assumed that democracy was irresistible, and that the question to be considered was, not whether it was good or evil in itself, but how we could best adapt ourselves to it. This is *ignava ratio*, the coward's argument, by which I hope this House will not be influenced.[1]

This was Robert Lowe, chief Liberal opponent of the working-class franchise in 1867, spitting into the wind. It is possible to sympathize with him; he was experiencing, as presumably most intelligent politicians must do sooner or later, the exasperating power of a pervasive contemporary cliché. In this case it was what served the nineteenth century as the matrix for many kinds of political opinion: the idea of a general historical process, guided by an inexorable inner principle of movement. The fashionable sciences of geology and biology supplied apt metaphors. There was Gladstone, for example, calling on geology to demonstrate what unscientific minds might have found dubious, that the irresistibility of a change was in proportion to the difficulty of noticing it: 'it is unobservable in detail, but as solid and undeniable as it is resistless in its essential character. It is like those movements in the crust of the earth which science tells us are even now going on in certain parts of the globe.'[2] In appealing to the historical process, the advocates of Reform in 1867, like their predecessors in 1832, were taking possession of the rhetorical high ground, which Lowe's constitutional picking and choosing, though itself expressed in a well-established vocabulary of utility, enriched by the vogue word of the fifties and sixties, 'efficiency', could not match. Lowe blamed Tocqueville, but though he was certainly the greatest single influence in shaping

[1] Robert Lowe, *Speeches and Letters on Reform* (London, 1867), 29
[2] Quoted in Alan Bullock and Maurice Shock, *The Liberal Tradition from Fox to Keynes* (London, 1956), 147

mid-Victorian notions of a developing democratic society, the inclination to conduct political argument by reference to a supposedly inevitable direction in history, evinced in the nature and tendency of modern society, was far older, and far more diffuse and deep-seated than could be attributed to any one writer.

It was an inclination which carried its own kind of intellectual dilemma for the would-be political agent of which Marx's 'Theses on Feuerbach' are only the best-known as well as the most gnomic formulation. It was not just that disgruntled liberals objected to having the world-historical process filched from them by democracy, though there is plenty of evidence for that: Maine in 1885 was still denouncing auto-suggestion and fatalism very much in the manner of Lowe in 1867.[3] But there was also a genuine dilemma. Mill has been aptly described as trying, in the early chapters of the essay on *Representative Government*, to escape the constrictions of a too rigorous commitment to the idea that the form of society determined the form of politics, and to restore at least some limited measure of autonomy and significance to political thought and initiative.[4] In his *Autobiography* we find him similarly puzzled: rescued from apathy partly by the notion that history has a pattern and a meaning, he then understandably became perturbed that one could perhaps not enjoy the comforts of determinism without its drawbacks.[5] It was an anxiety which could take various forms, philosophical or politically urgent. We find Mill's disciple John Morley, for example, in 1886, blaming the influence of 'the Historic Method' for 'latitudinarian acquiescence' and 'impoverished moral energy'· 'The historic conception is a reference of every state of society to a particular stage in the evolution of its general conditions', the result is that men become spectators of their own affairs and reforming initiative is disregarded.[6] It was not a very different argument from T H. Huxley's famous rejection of evolutionist social determinism in his 'Evolution and Ethics'

---

[3] Sir Henry Maine, *Popular Government* (2nd edn., London, 1886), pp. viii, 74.
[4] Stefan Collini, Donald Winch, and John Burrow, *That Noble Science of Politics: A Study in Nineteenth-century Intellectual History* (Cambridge University Press, 1983), essay IV (by Collini), 149 ff.
[5] J. S. Mill, *Autobiography*, ed. J. Stillinger (Oxford University Press, 1971), 102.
[6] John Morley, *On Compromise* (London, 1901, 1st edn., 1886), 28, 29, 30–1.

in 1893 Historical inevitability is a tricky polemical weapon, and brings comfort or irritation according to circumstances and the nature of one's hopes. We can see them both in the equivocations of one of the young liberal contributors to *Essays on Reform*, George Brodrick, who in answering Lowe disclaimed belief in political inevitability, while at the same time restating the case for reform as constitutional adjustment. The tendency to 'an equality of social conditions' discerned by Tocqueville,

> though no more inevitable than any other moral phenomenon, is one which a legislator must accept as a fact, because it is almost independent of legislation. The real question is, whether our representative system should be from time to time adjusted to the growing requirements of our social development, or should be employed as a barrier to retard progress.[7]

But a few years earlier, in an essay entitled 'Political Necessity', Brodrick had protested against political fatalism, diagnosing it as a distinctively modern *malaise*: nowadays 'the world seems to move of itself and nothing to remain for statesmanship but the diagnosis of its tendencies    wisdom is felt to consist in steering to that side where the stream runs strongest, in stealing a march on destiny by forestalling and adopting its designs' [8]

The dominance of 'society' over political forms, with the implied reduction of political initiative to adjustment, and the idea of a central line of inevitable historical transformation, were clichés, but their generality and pervasiveness made them tools with various uses; they could justify radicalism—because the contemplated changes were already implicit—or passivity; they could seem alarming or stifling. Leslie Stephen, for example, in *Essays on Reform*, uses them both to threaten and to reassure. Constitutional reform must come because the prior transformation of society requires it, but it is not alarming, because the working of political institutions cannot fail to reflect the underlying realities of society and manners: social deference will remain a potent force even when the working

---

[7] George Brodrick, 'The Utilitarian Argument Against Reform, As Stated by Mr Lowe', in *Essays on Reform* (London, 1867), 21–2.
[8] George Brodrick, *Political Studies* (London, 1879), 135.

class has the vote.[9] James Mill had made much the same point half a century before.[10]

We need now to turn back to consider some antecedents of and possible contrasts to these central notions of nineteenth-century political debate: the self-transformation of 'society', the notion that politics reflects rather than shapes it; and, as an aspect of this, as Stephen reminds us, the crucial influence of manners. But first, as a fixed point of comparison, it will be helpful to have a typical and comprehensive nineteenth-century formulation. In fact, of course, for so widespread and influential a cluster of ideas there can be no single definitive statement. But one which is certainly comprehensive and concise, as well as sufficiently typical is to be found in J. S. Mill's *Autobiography*; and it has the additional advantage that it attempts an explicit contrast with what he takes to be the older ideas on politics, now superseded. In a famous passage Mill sets out the 'new' theoretical assumptions about politics at which he had arrived by the early 1830s, in contrast to what, taking his father's *Essay on Government* as the model, he regards as the 'eighteenth-century', a priori deductive method. The new, nineteenth-century, and for Mill, it seems, almost exclusively Continental, doctrines he embraced, notably from the Saint-Simonians, are,

> that all questions of political institutions are relative, not absolute, and that different stages of human progress not only will have, but *ought* to have, different institutions; that government is always either in the hands, or passing into the hands, of whatever is the strongest power in society, and that what this power is, does not depend on institutions, but institutions on it; that any general theory or philosophy of politics supposes a previous theory of human progress, and that this is the same thing with a philosophy of history [11]

Mill's formula consists of a number of claims, and if we take it comprehensively, as a sketch for a political philosophy deduced from a highly coherent and deterministic conception of the course of human history, then we may concede that it

---

[9] Leslie Stephen, 'The Choice of Representatives by Popular Constituencies', in *Essays on Reform*.
[10] James Mill, *Essay on Government* (London, 1820).
[11] J. S. Mill, *Autobiography*, p. 97

is very largely, and certainly most typically—though perhaps not exclusively—a nineteenth-century way of thinking. But if we begin to take the formula to pieces and look at some of its components, we may begin to doubt whether they are either as novel or as foreign as he thinks they are. Among the neo-Harringtonian English and Scottish republicans of the late seventeenth and early eighteenth centuries, for example, the dependence of political power on the distribution of property in society was an axiom. As one of them, John Trenchard, put it, 'the first principle of all Power is property    this is natural Power, and will govern and constitute the political' The inferred prescription is spelt out; it is adjustment: 'the great secret of Politics is, nicely to watch and observe this Fluctuation and Change of natural Power, and to adjust the political to it by prudent Precautions and timely Remedies, and not to put Nature to the expense of Throws and Convulsions to do her own Work.'[12]

If we consider this as a typical statement, it could perhaps be misleading; a classical republican of Trenchard's kind was as likely to think of adjusting the social to the political; hankering, for example, for an agrarian law to prevent the further concentration of landed property, and so to preserve the economic base of the mass of independent freeholders on whom political liberty chiefly depended.[13] Of course, there are various differences between Mill's formulation and Trenchard's. The reference to property is explicit in the latter; Mill here is more ambiguous about the basis of power, though property figures largely, along with education and consciousness of common interest, in nineteenth-century Whig conceptions of a changing balance of social power presented in arguments for the extension of the franchise. But the most significant addition is Mill's reference to 'progress' He was right, of course, in making it central to the social and political

[12] John Trenchard and Thomas Gordon, in David L. Jacobson (ed.), *The English Libertarian Heritage* (New York, 1965), 211, 214.
[13] A striking example is Fletcher of Saltoun. See John Robertson, 'The Scottish Enlightenment at the limits of the Civic Tradition', in Istvan Hont and Michael Ignatieff (eds.), *Wealth and Virtue: The Shaping of Political Economy in the Scottish Enlightenment* (Cambridge University Press, 1983). Cf. e.g. Henry Neville, *Plato Redivivus* (1681), in Caroline Robbins (ed.), *Two English Republican Tracts* (Cambridge University Press, 1969), 99

speculations of his own time and not least of his own country, whether formally worked into a philosophy of history (or, as it would typically have been called later in the century, an account of social evolution) or functioning merely as a half-articulated premiss. In fact the historical qualifications we have been considering, to the way Mill introduces it, require us to see his claim about its origins as chronologically and geographically too limited, not as too extensive.

Taken in its broadest sense, Mill is speaking of the relation of the community organized in its explicit political aspect, as government and public law, to the subtler, sometimes tacit interconnections of social life. In the seventeenth and eighteenth centuries the latter had begun to be seen as a distinct category· 'civil society' Locke, in an age of revolution and threatened civil war, had distinguished civil society from political authority, in explaining how men might be without government yet not in a state of war, but his conception was unhistorical and unspecific. The relations of civil society, and its historical mutations, still remained to be picked out. One important step had been the emergence of the idea of the 'feudal' as a distinctive form of social organization, as lawyers came to recognize feudal law as belonging to a recent past, not entirely dead but certainly not covering the transactions of a commercial society [14] Another step was recognition of the ways in which commerce, the workings of the market, formed a distinct and intelligible set of relations, which could be systematically studied in what came to be called Political Economy Thus 'feudal' and 'commercial' became the most important categories, the two latest stages, of the sequence spoken of by the writers of the Scottish Enlightenment in the later eighteenth century as 'the history of Civil Society' It was a new kind of classification, not constitutional, dividing polities into monarchies, aristocracies, and democracies or republics, but social and economic. It raised, inevitably, the question how the two typologies, of polity and society, might be related, and

---

[14] For the discovery of 'feudalism', see J. G. A. Pocock, *The Ancient Constitution and the Feudal Law* (Cambridge University Press, 1957); on the legal significance of a concept of commercial society, see David Lieberman, 'The Legal Needs of a Commercial Society: The Jurisprudence of Lord Kames', in Hont and Ignatieff, *Wealth and Virtue*.

how society might influence political institutions or vice versa.¹⁵

The most obvious contrast between Mill and Trenchard is not one between a view of politics which stresses its relation to social change and one which sees political activity as simply autonomous and self-generating; it is primarily a contrast in evaluation. Mill, at that point at least, presents himself as an optimist willingly surrendering to the flow of social transformation ('not only will have, but ought to have') seen, without cavil, as 'progress' The characteristic stance of the early eighteenth-century republican Whig and of the Country Party opposition spokesman, who, following Bolingbroke's lead, took so much of their rhetoric from the neo-classical, civic-humanist, republican complex of ideas, was suspicious and pessimistic. This is because political life, the public life of the free citizen, the maintenance of the political liberty enjoyed in a balanced constitutional polity, is the primary good. The fluctuations in power and property, and the growth of opulence, are threats. The liberty it stresses is not negative freedom, freedom from interference, but free political participation as the highest life for man. 'Luxury', the product of opulence, diverts men from the exercise of patriotic virtue in the life of the polity into the leisured enjoyment of the pleasures of private life.¹⁶

Thanks to the efforts of a number of scholars we have now begun to gain some understanding of the complicated interrelations, in the middle and late eighteenth century, between the civic-humanist complex of values represented by the republican Whigs and the Country Party, and the newer set of values associated, above all in Scotland, with the concept of the progress of civil society The later eighteenth-century Scottish conception of the development of civil society from rudeness to refinement seems to revise the historical pessimism of the neo-classical, constitutionalist preoccupation with balance and the corrupting effects of luxury Instead of a way of thinking dominated by a constitutional typology inherited

---

[15] Pocock, 'Cambridge Paradigms and Scotch Philosophers', in Hont and Ignatieff, *Wealth and Virtue*.

[16] The classic study of 18th-cent. civic-humanist republican Whig and Country Party ideas is J. G. A. Pocock, *The Machiavellian Moment: Florentine Political Thought and the Atlantic Republican Tradition* (Princeton, 1975).

from Aristotle and Polybius, and modified by Montesquieu—monarchy, aristocracy, democracy, and republic—we have the central antithesis of feudal and commercial as the two latest stages of civil society Commercial society, seen as the characteristic form of modernity, is not a type of polity—there is no one particular form of constitution which alone is compatible with a polite and refined society—but a tissue of manners and modes of social behaviour, sometimes referred to by the new term 'civilization' [17]

This shift from polity to society, in the sense of at least the possibility of an insouciance about forms of constitution and a confident reliance on the effect of manners in softening and steadying the actions of various types of government, is most marked in Hume; it was one of the sources of his reputation for political cynicism. Certainly it is easy to see him as politically unclassifiable in eighteenth-century terms, which is why his contemporaries were outraged by him, and we can be grateful to Mr Duncan Forbes for his use of 'sceptical Whig',[18] though I may extend its use beyond what he would approve of.

Hume's coolness to the neo-classical political tradition was expressed in a profoundly influential contrast, still fundamental to Benjamin Constant and Macaulay in the 1820s, between the ancient and modern forms of liberty [19] In making it he was distancing himself from the strident neo-classical, political

[17] It is difficult to present the antithesis outlined in the above paragraph without over-simplification. In fact, studies of leading figures of the Scottish Enlightenment have made it clear that these two conceptions were typically locked in a complicated interplay which is somewhat different in each author. See e.g. Donald Winch, *Adam Smith's Politics: An Essay in Historiographic Revision* (Cambridge University Press, 1978), and the essays in Hont and Ignatieff, *Wealth and Virtue*, esp. Pocock's general discussion of this question: 'Cambridge Paradigms and Scotch Philosophers.'

[18] For Forbes's uses of 'scientific', 'vulgar', and 'sceptical' Whiggism, see Duncan Forbes, *Hume's Philosophical Politics* (Cambridge University Press, 1975), ch. 5, and 'Sceptical Whiggism, Commerce and Liberty', in A. S. Skinner and T Wilson (eds.), *Essays on Adam Smith* (Oxford University Press, 1976).

[19] In saying this I do not mean to imply that the distinction is as fully elaborated in Hume as in Constant; in the former it is one current in a very complex body of writing, in the latter an explicitly propounded thesis. It is not possible here, of course, even to hint at the tensions and complexities in Hume's work, which present formidable problems of interpretation. For Constant's relations to the Scottish Enlightenment, see Biancamaria Fontana, 'The Shaping of Modern Liberty: Commerce and Civilization in the writings of Benjamin Constant', *Annales Benjamin Constant*, 5 (1985).

moralizing of the 'Country' opposition but he was also unconsciously forging a weapon for the future against the neoclassical republicanism of revolutionary France. France, in Hume's essays, offers a largely benign case of the distinction between polity and society France has not a free constitution but she has most of the makings of a free society in the modern sense; her citizens enjoy private liberty and security though they lack political rights. The free citizen of the classical *polis*, however, enjoyed little personal security or liberty; his time, life, and goods were at the disposal of the state.[20]

In the generation after Hume, of course, though the categories remained the same, the French example told very differently The new Whig wisdom declared that the Revolution was the revenge of society on polity· the old French political regime had become drastically divorced from French society; the progress of civil society had outgrown the French monarchy [21] The Revolution, in this view, was in the long run necessary to restore the relation between society and polity, but in the short term the balance tilts the other way The doctrinaire republicanism of the Revolution, inspired partly by the examples, so influential on eighteenth-century minds, of Sparta and early Rome, could be seen as a conscious attempt to impose the values of the *polis*, the principles of political virtue and patriotism learnt from Livy, Plutarch, and Rousseau, on a civilized and modern society Macaulay clearly recognized the analogy between the French cult of republican Rome and that of English republican Whigs of a hundred years earlier, such as Molesworth, Molyneaux, and Fletcher of Saltoun, and despised it in both forms.[22]

Central to the contrast in Hume and Macaulay between an ancient political 'liberty' without private freedom, and the space

---

[20] Hume, 'Of Civil Liberty', in *Essays Moral, Political and Literary*, eds. T H. Green and T H. Grose, 2 vols. (London, 1875), vol. 1, esp. 161. Cf. 'Of Commerce', pp. 287–99, and 'Of the Populousness of Ancient Nations', pp. 381–443. Earlier formulations of the notion of liberty as modern are to be found in the defenders of Walpole's ministry against Bolingbroke and the Country Party opposition.

[21] Fontana, *Rethinking the Politics of Commercial Society: The Edinburgh Review 1802–1832* (Cambridge University Press, 1985), ch. 1.

[22] Thomas Babington Macaulay, 'Plutarch and his School', *The Works of Lord Macaulay*, ed. Lady Trevelyan, 8 vols. (London, 1897), v 137–9 Cf. ibid. 40, 619, 635.

created in a modern society for the free play of individual choice secured by law and property, but distinct from political participation, is Hume's notion of the 'mildness', the tolerance and politeness of modern manners, which went with commerce and the enjoyment of opulence, and which formed a part of what Macaulay was more comprehensively and loudly to celebrate as civilization and progress. It was a view, and an acceptance of modernity, which made the cult of the *polis* as a political model an anachronism.

Of course there is another, and in a sense the defining, aspect of modern society when conceived of as essentially commercial. No one is likely to be in danger of not being told that Adam Smith had a concept of the market. But the category of commercial society included much more than the market. The notion that there are laws governing the interaction of individual human activity, exemplified above all in the market, which produce immense, unplanned, long-term consequences, was a fundamental concept of the Scottish Enlightenment. It was relevant in helping to reverse the priority attributed respectively to polity and society Political action designed to influence social behaviour came to seem necessarily more complex and circumspect; instead of the authority of patriotic political moralism, we are invited, in some areas at least, to recognize a gap, a disjunction between the moral quality of action and its remoter social consequences. In particular, of course, the notion of 'luxury', the classical political moralists' *bête noire*, and its supposedly pernicious consequences for political liberty, becomes at least equivocal, if the modern form of individual liberty and security is associated with the opulence that is the result of industriousness and commerce.

But we have to be careful not to overstate here. Because the idea of commercial society was a pregnant one, it is tempting to anticipate, and to impose essentially nineteenth-century models of economic *laissez-faire*, only partially useful even where they best apply, to eighteenth-century notions of commercial society Aspects of the latter, indeed, caused unease to its exponents, yet in its most positive aspect it implied not merely a set of social relations but a complex of values, significantly different both from Catonic, republican virtue and self-denial, and from the equivalent but differently focused rigours of the vulgarized nineteenth-century commercial ethos: the creed commonly associated with Samuel Smiles and Matthew Arnold's Philistines.

Eighteenth-century neo-classical patriotism and Smilesian self-help, in fact, were both grounded in an austere strenuousness, though one exalted the public and political dimension of life, and the other resolutely ignored it and tended to suspect all government as 'meddling'. Both, however, suspected luxury, though one called it corruption and the other extravagance; both extolled 'independence'. They were ethics which believed in keeping the screws tight and energy concentrated by compression. One became the creed of a disgruntled political opposition, the other that of a provincial manufacturing and commercial class with its roots in religious dissent. By contrast, eighteenth-century notions of civility and improvement were both substantially derived from and deeply infused in English Establishment Whiggism,[23] a culture which, consciously on the latter's part, stretched from Addison to Macaulay; it left its residues in Victorian notions of the gentleman and the liberal education which formed him, later severely modified by more Spartan conceptions of character and team-spirit fostered by compulsory games, and finding their natural expression in public service.

The contrasts can best be seen in the different attitudes to leisure. In civic-humanist republican rhetoric it was despised and suspected as a corruption and luxury, a self-indulgent diversion from the exercise of public virtue; leisure, initially *otium*, continued to carry its suggestion of the otiose.[24] But in what we may loosely call the ethics of Establishment

[23] I follow H. T Dickinson (*Liberty and Property: Political Ideology in Eighteenth-century Britain* (London, 1977) ) in using the term 'Establishment Whig' As I shall use it, applied chiefly to the later 18th cent., it has a convenient looseness which overcomes the difficulty in referring to 'Court' or 'Ministerialist' Whigs after the accession of George III. Blackstone could perhaps be allowed to define the category. It expresses something more commonplace, with less intellectual penetration and sociological detachment, than Forbes's uses of 'scientific' and 'sceptical' as adjectives for a distinctly Scottish kind of Whiggism. It stands, however, in a similar relation of opposition to the 'Country' (or 'vulgar') Whig, and to 'radical Whigs' (for the Lockian ideas, especially among Dissenters, tending towards manhood suffrage, from the time of the American War onwards). In the early 19th cent. I shall speak of the Whiggism of the *Edinburgh Review* sort as 'reforming' or 'progressive' Whiggism.

[24] I am indebted to Quentin Skinner for pointing out this connection.

Whiggism it came to be seen as a vital aspect of improvement and civilization, indispensable to the polite, disinterested, and tolerant sociability which polished manners, broadened opinions, and enhanced life. It was in a sense both private and public; social but not political. As the former it is easily distinguishable from the sentimental images of the nineteenth-century cult of domesticity, contrasted, as a refuge, with a hard world of commercial competition: the iron laws of the market and the soft armchairs of home; the returned economic warrior brought his slippers by a flutter of dutiful daughters; 'Home Sweet Home' on the piano and the curtains gratefully drawn against the dusk. Instead, of course, we have to think of an image of well-being and the good life, not as consumption (of which Adam Smith is notably contemptuous)[25] or as seclusion, but as the conscious—one might even say conscientious—cultivation of the pleasures of a tolerant, rational, and improving sociability From pastoralism through feudalism to commerce as the history of civil society was also the history of manners from rudeness and barbarism to politeness and refinement, and it was in the latter that the value inhering in the story chiefly resided.[26]

The underlying conception of stages in the development of civil society was a distinctively Scottish one (it is a standing temptation to pronounce 'Rudeness to Refinement' in a Morningside accent). But of course the ethic from which the moral judgement embodied in it derives was more widely diffused.[27] To fill out a little the moral suggestions of an ethic which, as its critics complained, was always in danger of eliding the distinction between morals and manners, we might consider for a moment the connotations of that common eighteenth-century English usage of 'the Town' for London, or rather that part of it in which everybody who was anybody knew or at least knew of everybody else. It was often satirized as a

---

[25] 'For what purpose is all the toil and bustle of this world? What is the end of avarice and ambition, of the pursuit of wealth of power and preeminence? Is it to supply the necessities of nature? The wages of the meanest labourer can supply them.' *Theory of Moral Sentiments* (11th edn., London, 1812), 81.

[26] Nicholas Phillipson, 'Adam Smith as Civic Moralist', in Hont and Ignatieff, *Wealth and Virtue*, passim.

[27] See e.g. Edward Alan Bloom and Lillian D Bloom, *Joseph Addison's Social Animal* (London, 1971).

theatre of illusion for the satisfaction of vanity, from the vantage-point of a neo-classical pessimism which denounced luxury as the ruin of the commonwealth. Yet it was, nevertheless (rather than Parliament, though it included it, or the court or the camp or the university), the school of life where the individual improved and refined himself; where the rough edges of social encounter were smoothed and made agreeable; and where ideas were exchanged in an atmosphere of tolerant civility [28] It was still restricted enough — and it came to have numerous provincial counterparts — for intimacy and even for something of the intensity, the feuds, the aching concern for reputation, of the classical *polis*, but without its dangers and sacrifices. In this world, 'society' was a word tinged with expectations of enjoyment; it meant 'company' 'Social' was an adjective whose sense of approbation included the moral. When Gibbon, for example, speaks of early Christian zeal as 'unsocial', or Macaulay uses the same term of the Covenanters, the weight of disapproval is heavy One of the chief enemies of a tolerant sociability was fanaticism or, in the eighteenth-century sense, 'enthusiasm' Gibbon lived long enough to see the outbreak of the French Revolution, and made the obvious analogy with the early Christian zealots; the revolutionaries were 'the fanatic missionaries of sedition' [29] Hume's violent reaction to the Wilkite agitation ('the frenzy of liberty') leaves no doubt that he would have fully shared Gibbon's response;[30] he could have made a similar identification with the Puritan revolutionaries on whom he himself had written.

Hume's Scottish emphasis on the progress of society and manners — so that it seemed the form of polity might be monarchical or republican with little effect on the individual, so long as manners were mild, laws observed, and private life

---

[28] Sheldon Rothblatt, *Tradition and Change in English Liberal Education* (London, 1976), chs. 2-8.

[29] Edward Gibbon, *Memoirs of My Life and Writings*, ed. Georges A. Bonnard (London, 1966), 185. As Pocock says, 'there was room for another analysis, which Gibbon might perhaps have written: that of the fanaticism of civic virtue' 'Gibbon and the Late Enlightenment', *Virtue, Commerce and History: Essays on Political Thought and History Chiefly in the Eighteenth century* (Cambridge University Press, 1985), 156.

[30] Ernest Campbell Mossner, *The Life of David Hume* (2nd edn., Oxford University Press, 1980), 485, 486.

and property respected—implied a kind of confidence in, or acceptance of, the historical process, and hence of the nature of modernity It did not look in desperation for an Archimedean point, the social contract or the original principles of the constitution, on which to ground all political legitimacy On the other hand, it was not—it is tempting to say not yet—historicist in the determinist fashion of nineteenth-century philosophies of history It did not extrapolate to a remote future, or speak of inexorable laws of social development, but only of intelligible principles of change in what had occurred, with outcomes on the whole desirable though not without their associated difficulties. Yet there was, of course, confidence, of a kind we find also in Burke's speeches on America, in what both Hume and Smith call 'the natural system', in the free spontaneous agency of men's ordinary motives and activities.[31] Its opposite was 'violent' or 'artificial' As Hume says in his essay on 'Commerce', 'ancient policy was violent, and contrary to the more natural and usual course of things' [32] A polity like Sparta, or the early Roman republic, was produced by special historical circumstances—the theme Macaulay would later take up—and not for imitation.[33]

The effect of Hume's critique was to present the civic virtue of the ancient republics not, as it figured in Country Party rhetoric and was later to do in that of the French revolutionaries, as supremely exemplary but as aberrant and artificial. It was a criticism Burke applied with relish to the political language of his contemporaries in both its forms. It was no sound insurance for constitutional liberty to rely on 'a rare and heroic virtue' [34] Burke inherited the modern Whig's confidence in the civilizing effect of manners even if he tended to make them traditional rather than, like Hume and Smith,

---

[31] Cf. Hume: in general 'sovereigns must take mankind as they find them, and cannot pretend to introduce any violent change in their principles & ways of thinking. A long course of time, with a variety of accidents and circumstances are requisite to produce those great revolutions, which so much diversify the face of human affairs.' *Essays*, i. 292.     [32] Ibid. 291.

[33] Ibid. 291-2. Cf. Macaulay, 'Machiavelli', and 'Plutarch and his School', in *Works*, vol. v

[34] Burke's point here was the need for payment of office holders. 'Economical Reform', in *The Writings and Speeches of Edmund Burke*, 12 vols. (London, 1900), ii. 335.

the moral dimension of commercial society· 'whilst manners remain entire, they will correct the vices of law, and soften it at length to their own temper.'[35] It was not government that regenerated society, but the civilizing influences of society that modified the exactions of governments. The contrast between the violent and arbitrary, epitomized in the French Revolution, and the natural and ordinary course of society, was to be a long-standing Whig and Liberal antithesis. We find it, for example, in Acton, a hundred years after Hume, using almost the same words as Burke; Jacobinism was essentially at war with French society· 'The democratic constitution required to be upheld by violence, not only against foreign arms, but against the state of society and the nature of things.'[36]

But the Burkian and nineteenth-century Whig concept of working with, not against, the grain of society and manners allowed for much complexity in the latter; it is certainly not reducible to the individualism of market economies, though it could include it, nor did it reduce government to a nullity For Burke, government was the constant fine tuning of the interaction of a mass of diverse social interests which were, as he told his Bristol electors, 'various, multiform, and intricate' It was a version of the idea of 'unintended consequences' but the inference was only to an extent a *laissez-faire* one. Parliament was the essential mediator: 'all these widespread interests must be considered,—must be compared,—must be reconciled, if possible . the machine of a free constitution is no simple thing, but as intricate and as delicate as it is valuable A constitution made up of balanced powers must ever be a critical thing.' Hume, in his sparer vocabulary, had said something similar.[37]

In Burke's writings the polity/society distinction often seems unhelpful, because in a healthy state he regards government and public institutions both as emanations of, and also as

---

[35] 'Letter to the Sheriffs of Bristol' (1777), ibid. 202.
[36] Lord Acton, *The History of Freedom and Other Essays*, ed. J. N. Figgis (London, 1909), 264. Cf. Burke, 'they think everything unworthy of the name of public virtue, unless it indicates violence on the private', 'Regicide Peace', in *Writings and Speeches*, v. 312.
[37] Burke, 'Conclusion of the Poll' (1774), in *Writings and Speeches*, ii. 97 Cf. Hume, 'Of the Rise and Progress of the Arts & Sciences', in *Essays*, i. 185.

shaping influences in, society It is partly because he tried to speak of them as fused that his language takes on a mystical tinge, trying to express a subtly reciprocal communion for which ready-made words scarcely existed. Yet the two central political events of his life, the American and French Revolutions, forced him to consider them as conceptually, because really, distinct. The British government, relying on an abstract constitutional legality rather than unforced community of sentiment, and attempting to impose its will on an incalculably developing colonial society, was making visible the same dichotomy as the French revolutionaries, later, when he presents them as a government bent on violently reshaping society to a preconceived model. In America, colonial society has its own principle of energy· 'the colonies in general owe little or nothing to any care of ours, and they are not squeezed into this happy form by the constraints of watchful and suspicious government, but through a wise and salutary neglect, a generous nature has been suffered to take her own way to perfection.'[38]

The French government in the 1790s offers the opposite example of the same lesson. In France the state has 'dominion over minds by proselytism, over bodies by arms The riches of convention disappear', 'the property is in complete subjection and nothing rules but the mind of desperate men' [39] The relations between polity and society, properly characterized by an almost tremulous sensitivity, mediated through numerous subsidiary authorities, and to be appreciated only by a combination of experience and the utmost resources of political imagination and tact, are here seen as reduced to violence and strident manipulation.

Yet, of course, at the extreme limit of Burke's outrage the diagnosis of the French Revolution assumed the character of social pessimism and a deep distrust of the possible movement of civil society, which, in the central role it assigned to the French National Debt, echoed earlier civic-humanist aversions. The revolutionaries are, in this view, as J G. A. Pocock has recently pointed out, not, indeed, a commercial bourgeoisie,

---

[38] Burke, 'Conciliation' (1775), in *Writings and Speeches*, ii. 117–18.
[39] 'Letters on a Regicide Peace', 2, ibid. v 375–7

but a distinctive creation or perversion of modern commercial society none the less: a 'moneyed interest' based on paper credit, in alliance with a rootless intelligentsia whose medium is the press. It is emphatically not a 'modern' or 'progressive' Whig diagnosis, in the sense that the Revolution arises not from a disjunction between the constitution and the progress of civil society, but from something like a demonic perversion in the development of that society This had come about because the essential civilizing agency of 'manners' had lost contact with its roots in religion and 'chivalry' Pocock suggests that it is here that we should see the link between Burke and the Coleridgian and religious critique of the 'mechanistic' philosophy of commercial society, which became a staple ingredient of the Tory Radicalism of the first part of the nineteenth century The counter to the evils of commercial society is a responsible aristocracy, an endowed clerisy, and a national church.[40]

But in the early years of the nineteenth century the main intellectual alternative to a confident Whig pragmatism was not yet such a critique, and was no longer a neo-classical 'patriotism', but a rationalistic radicalism, derived to a significant extent from Locke. A characteristic seventeenth-century despair of finding sure grounds for knowledge, morality, or even peace, in existing custom and consensus, had issued through Locke not only in the concept of an original social contract but in an epistemology which made the individual's sensations the only ultimate reality In the early nineteenth century the politically formidable offshoot of that epistemology, and the associationist psychological doctrines which formed part of it, was Benthamism. The suspicion of custom and received opinion as prejudice became the radical Benthamite view that English institutions and established political culture were a sham, a nightmare of delusive fictions, whose function was to protect and disguise the sinister vested interests which controlled society for their own ends, and which contaminated not only politics but language itself. Nineteenth-century intellectual Whiggism was obliged to define itself not

---

[40] Pocock, 'The Political Economy of Burke's analysis of the French Revolution', in *Virtue, Commerce and History*, pp. 193-212.

only against Tory intransigence but in opposition to the Benthamite challenge.

Macaulay struck not at the periphery but at the centre of the Philosophic Radicals' position when, in attacking James Mill, he mocked their addiction to jargon and their distrust of ordinary language. Bentham's cultivation of a distinctive, to his contemporaries ungainly, and in his later years occasionally almost impenetrable, idiom, was an attempt at a radical cleansing of the instrument of thought. It was in its own way as much an attempt to step outside history and society to eternally valid principles of judgement as the Paineite attempt to do so with the concept of universal natural rights. Bentham's self-created jargon expressed a deep distrust of the untidiness, the flexible, emotionally charged imprecision, of the everyday political and moral language of his time.

The nineteenth-century Whig, on the other hand, embraced the common language of educated society and public life as the expression of bonds of sentiment, habit, civilized manners that transcended the political, and in fact largely controlled the effects of any particular given political constitution, as they also qualified and restrained the pursuit of self-interest by individuals. As Macaulay said in his attack on James Mill, 'civilised men pursuing their own happiness in a social state are not Yahoos fighting for carrion' [41] The important thing was not truisms about men's pursuit of self-interest, but the habitual restraints on it they voluntarily accepted. To the Whig of the *Edinburgh Review*, 'ordinary', as when speaking of ordinary language, ordinary good sense, was a term of strong commendation, and utilitarian jargon at best garnished the obvious—that government existed to promote the general happiness—with an unnecessary, implausible, and uncouth affectation of precision.[42] When Francis Jeffrey attacked Benthamite utilitarian ethics he made the point that our acceptance of its central principle, the principle of utility, must be dependent on its congruity with our prior moral intuitions, and that when we find the dictates of utility inconsistent with

---

[41] Macaulay, in Jack Lively and John Rees, *Utilitarian Logic and Politics: James Mill's 'Essay on Government' and Macaulay's Critique and the Ensuing Debate* (Oxford University Press, 1978), 117   [42] Ibid. 100.

those, we reject them. Jeffrey drew a robustly commonsensical conclusion:

> The common impressions of morality, the vulgar distinctions of right and wrong, virtue and vice, are perfectly sufficient to direct and conduct the individual, and the judgement of the legislator, without any reference to the nature or origin of these distinctions. In many respects indeed, we conceive them to be fitter for these purposes than Mr Bentham's oracles of utility [43]

The *Edinburgh* Whigs' confidence in the ordinary had a philosophical basis, in the epistemological and ethical doctrines of the Common Sense school of philosophy stemming from Thomas Reid.[44] But it rested on a broader cultural foundation, and on another kind of confidence than the philosophical: Jeffrey, in fact, was as condescending in reviewing Reid as he generally was about philosophy [45] The references to the ordinary, the accepted, the sensible, were appeals to the political culture and civilized values they shared with their readers. The prospects for the pragmatic reforms for which the *Edinburgh Review*'s kind of Whiggism stood were presumably good for precisely the same reasons as made them necessary The constitution and the administration of government was, in a significant degree, out of phase with— behind, they would have said—society, and needed adjustment. There was nothing revolutionary about appealing to society to create the pressure to restore polity What would be revolutionary would be attempting to transform society by political means—Jacobinism—or the Utilitarians' tactical severance of politics from the influences of civilization by a radical theoretical individualism, and a repudiation of the linguistic and habitual suggestiveness of an inherited political culture. The early nineteenth-century progressive Whig, speaking of common sense and adjustment, implied the priority of society over polity

Of course, the reforming impulse took in much more than

---

[43] Written in 1804. Francis Jeffrey, *Contributions to the Edinburgh Review* (London, 1853), 618.
[44] S. A. Grave, *The Scottish Philosophy of Common Sense* (Oxford University Press, 1960).
[45] e.g. his review of Stewart on Reid (1806), *Contributions to the Edinburgh Review*, p. 623.

strictly constitutional questions, and allowed for tactical alliances with the Philosophic Radicals. But the *Edinburgh* Whigs, though Tories might not always have given them credit for it, tried to hold a balance between bureaucratic zeal and tenderness to existing interests, which was the form, from the 1820s to the 1870s, that the government/society dichotomy chiefly assumed. And, of course, they differed from the Philosophic Radicals over the constitution, both in rejecting the abstract method of argument by which James Mill made the case for democracy, and in rejecting the democratic conclusion itself. Whigs came to favour a concept of adjustment which incorporated and amplified the later eighteenth-century Burkian conception of a balanced representation of interests.[46]

There was some necessary difference of emphasis here from some of their Scottish intellectual forebears, particularly Hume, whom they sometimes criticized sharply Hume's appearance of constitutional indifference—the distinction between barbarian arbitrariness and modern mildness overrode that between types of constitution when speaking of the modern form of private liberty—had been seen as eccentric and reprehensible by contemporaries. In the immediate aftermath of the French Revolution such indifference was no longer possible: civil society had overthrown an ancient polity, and then a revolutionary regime had seen itself as charged with the regeneration of society and manners. The task of the Whig reared in the Scottish intellectual milieu, whose fundamental explanatory category was the history of civil society, was clearly now to understand what had occurred,[47] as Hume had earlier attempted to explain the English Civil War. A continuing long-term optimism had to come to terms with anxieties centred not only, as was standard in the Whig tradition, on the stealthy encroachment of executive power, but on the possibility of revolution and the necessity for preservative reform. The result was a distinctively modern form of Whig constitutionalism and a sociological diagnosis of revolution.

But the Whig had to fight on several fronts, against Tory

---

[46] e.g. the review of Burdett's Reform proposal (by James Mackintosh), *Edinburgh Review*, 14 (1809), no. 28, pp. 184–5.
[47] Fontana, *Rethinking the Politics of Commercial Society*, ch. 1.

timidity and against radical rationalism and utopianism; it is easy, too, to anticipate the declining influence of the Crown and therefore to underrate the importance attached by Whigs to a continuing suspicion of the threat it represented to constitutional liberty So long as that threat was seen as a real one, as we shall see in a moment in Jeffrey, the civic humanists' concept of patriotic virtue would continue to reverberate in the language of the Whig, despite the inhibitions produced by the French Revolution. And between Tory passivity and radical over-optimism it was necessary to strike a middle way which included a balanced estimate of the relative importance of government and society Political forms had to be seen to matter, but not to be able to accomplish everything. To concede the latter would be to allow too much to the radicals' a priori arguments for an ideally reconstructed constitution, based on a theory of universal human nature; all beneficial change, for the progressive Whig, must be related to the actual state of society But to play the card of 'social forces' and 'manners' alone might seem to concede too much to political quietism, declaring the form of the constitution a matter of indifference and political reform a matter of no urgency In Macaulay's attack on James Mill we see him trying to steer between these alternatives and his opponent trying to convict him of political quietism.[48] The solution, for the early nineteenth-century Whig, was, of course, a notion of constitutional adjustment, peacefully restoring the relation between polity and society which the progress of civil society might disturb, and avoiding the possibility of a violent readjustment by, as Trenchard had said, 'throws and convulsions', as society took its revenge on a decayed polity which no longer expressed the stage of civilization it had reached. This was the argument Macaulay presented to the House of Commons in the debates on the First Reform Act, when he offered the examples of England in the seventeenth century and France in the 1780s as polities which had failed to adjust in time, and he did so in terms of a conception of history directly borrowed, it seems, from Hume

---

[48] Lively and Rees, *Utilitarian Logic*, pp. 206-8, 134-6. Cf. Dugald Stewart, quoted by Winch in Collini, Winch, and Burrow, *That Noble Science*, p. 41 n. 32.

and the Scottish Enlightenment's notion of the history of the history of civil society

But perhaps the most interesting moment, the closest theoretical fusion, as it were, of the two traditions, Whig constitutionalism and Scottish sociology, is provided by Francis Jeffrey, in several articles in the *Edinburgh Review* The first we need to attend to is his review of Fox's history of the 1688 Revolution, published in 1808. Jeffrey there makes a direct attack on Humean constitutional indifference and the emphasis on private liberty, from a position which is Foxite, Whig constitutionalist, in its doctrine, and contains strong civic-humanist echoes in its language. 'Private happiness, it is observed, has but little dependence on the nature of the government. The oppressions of monarchs and demagogues are nearly equal in degree.' Therefore, it is claimed we may as well 'occupy ourselves with the many innocent and pleasant pursuits that are allowed under all governments' Jeffrey attributes to Hume the blame 'for the prevalence of this Epicurean and ignoble strain of sentiment in this country' But in fact the doctrine is false: 'neither liberal nor even gainful pursuits can be carried out with advantage where there is no political freedom.' For the security of political freedom we must look, as always in the Whig tradition, to the jealous maintenance of the balance of the constitution.[49]

The whole of this article on the lessons of 1688 is strongly civic-humanist in tone, though it combines this with a distinctively Scottish confidence in the development of civil society Liberty 'is as hard to keep as to win', and it is the innate tendency of power to encroach.[50] The great danger therefore is complacency and the increase in luxury and patronage.[51] It is not only that the constitutional security for our liberty is endangered by apathy; there is the danger of forgetting 'our higher vocation of free citizens',[52] while 'the consciousness of independence is a *great enjoyment in itself*'[53] Traditional Country Party anxieties are blended with the reassurance supposedly provided by the growth and diffusion of opulence

---

[49] Francis Jeffrey, *Contributions to the Edinburgh Review*, p. 245.
[50] Ibid. 244.    [51] Ibid. 245.    [52] Ibid. 243.
[53] Ibid. 246. Italics original.

in civil society Thus, trade has made us luxurious, 'and he who is both needy and luxurious, holds his independence on a very precarious tenure'.[54] But to counteract 'these enervating and depressing causes' we have had

> the increasing opulence of the lower and middling orders of the people, naturally leading them to aspire to greater independence, and improving their education and general intelligence, and thus, public opinion which is in all countries the great operating check upon authority had become more extreme and more enlightened.[55]

What began as something like a civic-humanist republican sermon has turned at this point into something distinctively modern; the Foxite text is being expounded by a reforming son of the Scottish Enlightenment and a pupil of Dugald Stewart.[56]

Whig constitutionalism set in the context of a distinctively Scottish conception of the history of civil society, the two being linked by the concept of public opinion, is more fully expounded by Jeffrey in an article on government in 1812. There he offers a sketch of constitutional development written as a piece of Scottish speculative or conjectural universal history· the history of civil society Government—this was a Humean point which had become a cliché—always rests on consent, that is, on public opinion. Even a military despot is dependent on retaining the obedience of his troops. But the forms of public opinion, and the ways it is monitored and translated into political authority, vary according to the stage in the development of society The power of opinion manifested in the loyalty of the barbarian war band is more unstable and irregular than that of a feudal aristocracy with its armed retainers; the latter, again, is different from the diffusion of the power of concerted opinion found in a modern society, with its towns, newspapers, and speed of communications.[57]

But the check is not automatic. Maintaining the constitution in health still crucially matters; the *nature* of the checks on government is determined by 'the structure of society in each

---

[54] Ibid. 245.    [55] Ibid. 246.
[56] See Winch, 'The System of the North: Dugald Stewart and his Pupils', in Collini, Winch, and Burrow, *That Noble Science*, essay I.
[57] Jeffrey, *Contributions to the Edinburgh Review*, 729 Cf. for Dugald Stewart, Winch, in Collini, Winch, and Burrow, *That Noble Science*, 34.

particular nation', but how they operate, whether beneficially, 'with ease and safety', whether they are regular, orderly, and mild, or destructive, depends on the appropriateness of the way they are politically organized and expressed.[58] If law is the pressure government exerts on society, public opinion, with the ultimate sanction of rebellion behind it, is the pressure society exerts on government. But without an adequate transmitter for that pressure, in a parliament representative of 'the views of all considerable classes of the people  the danger of great convulsions will unfortunately become greater exactly in proportion as the body of the people become more wealthy and intelligent' [59] This had been the case of France.[60]

The notion of constitutional adjustment was the central Whig platitude of the first half of the nineteenth century, as the concept of restoration, returning the constitution to its original principles, had been that of the first half of the eighteenth. Changes in the balance of property were still seen as having constitutional implications, but it was necessary to work with, not against, the grain of history But though the French example remained monitory, it was increasingly accompanied, in discussions of the relative force exerted by politics on society, and of society and manners on the working of political systems, by the very different example of America, and the great democratic experiment being conducted in the United States in the age of Andrew Jackson and after.[61] In the debates surrounding the 1867 Reform Act, unlike that of 1832, it was America, and to a secondary extent the British Colonies, rather than France, which was seen as relevant. Revolution, in 1867, was a remote and implausible possibility; no intolerable social pressure was available to justify constitutional innovation. But foreseeing the probable nature of democracy in Britain was the central issue, and the United States offered the most obvious indicator [62]

---

[58] Jeffrey, *Contributions to the Edinburgh Review*, p. 728.
[59] Ibid. 731.   [60] Ibid. 732.
[61] See David P Crook, *American Democracy in English Politics 1815-1850* (Oxford University Press, 1965).
[62] Lowe, by his denunciations, had placed the working of democracy in America, and to a secondary extent in Australia, at the centre of the debate over the franchise, and the contributors to *Essays on Reform* had to take up the challenge: Goldwin Smith contributed an article on American politics, C. H. Pearson one on Australia, but America also figured as an important example in other essays.

The question was how far the different social structure and less egalitarian manners in Britain might modify the innate tendencies of democratic government, and indeed what those tendencies were. Was it American society and manners which gave a special character to American democratic politics, or did those politics create at least the manners, if not the structure, of the society? It was an argument one could run several ways, depending on one's sympathies. Either America demonstrated the virtues of democracy, or the vices of American democracy derived from its being American rather than its being a democracy.[63] Alternatively, American society was sound, but its politics were deplorable, either because of the special conditions created in New York and Boston by recent immigration,[64] or because democratic politics prevented good men from standing for election. Democracy in Britain would be better because it would be modified by the influence of a greater civility (or deference) and cultivation in manners.[65] Democracy in Britain would be worse because in America there was unlimited cheap land—this was the argument used by James Mackintosh and others—while Britain's population was confined, urban, and divided along lines of class.[66] All circumstances were special, and the essence of democracy continued to be elusive.[67] The American example could be trimmed to suit any political taste. In the absence of comparative controls, the new test case for the relations of polity and society proved nothing.

But it was seldom that the case of America was dismissed as altogether irrelevant, and Tocqueville's *Democracy in America* was one of the shaping influences on mid-Victorian liberalism, ensuring that democracy was seen in terms of

---

[63] Crook, *American Democracy*, e.g. pp. 117, 182.
[64] Ibid. 60. Cf. Leslie Stephen and O. A. Rutson in *Essays on Reform*, pp. 99-100, 284-5.
[65] English deference formed an important part of the reassurance about reform Stephen offered his readers in his contribution to *Essays on Reform*: 'On the Choice of Representatives by Popular Constituencies', cf. Rutson, ibid. 285-6.
[66] Crook, *American Democracy*, pp. 23-4, 79, 90.
[67] A point made by McCulloch and by J. S. Mill; see Crook, *American Democracy*, pp. 81, 182 n. 1. For Bryce's always deferred attempts to isolate the democratic essence, see Collini in Collini, Winch, and Burrow, *That Noble Science*, p. 243.

manners as well as constitutions, and that the force of egalitarian public opinion would be seen as a central feature.[68] The notion of American 'democratic manners' called for an appraisal that was moral and aesthetic as much as sociological and political; it was a question not of what American government might do but of what one might think of Americans. In so far as the character of constitutional debate had changed between 1832 and 1867, it was partly because of the increased prominence and equivocality of the American example, partly because of the distinctive political circumstances of 1867 reform in response to little discernible pressure. Lowe, in particular, having called their bluff, it was necessary for intellectual liberal supporters of an extended franchise to make a case that owed as much to morality as to necessity and the argument for adjustment.

It is true Gladstone was felt to have made a false step in referring to the franchise as a 'right' The echo of the discredited language of natural rights—now often thought of as distinctively French, despite its Lockian pedigree—was embarrassing.[69] But there were other moral idioms available: Comtist and Christian Socialist notions of co-operation and 'brotherhood', the Mazzinian nationalist rhetoric of patriotism and self-sacrifice, as well as more traditionally English, and Tocquevillian, ideas of self-government and education through the experience of political participation.[70] All these, though the latter had formed part of the language of the progressive Whig, gave the advanced Liberalism of the sixties, represented by *Essays on Reform*, a more idealistic, egalitarian, and even at times republican character than earlier Whig notions of mild and orderly government, secured by flexible constitutional adjustment and an adequate representation of diverse social interests.[71] The case for reform was presented, at least in part, in terms of political participation being itself a good, a field

---

[68] On Tocqueville's influence in England, see Crook, *American Democracy*, ch. v, and Seymour Drescher, *Tocqueville in England* (Cambridge, Mass., 1964), 217-21.   [69] *Essays on Reform*, pp. 10, 11, 65-6.

[70] On the importance of the example of Italian nationalism and Mazzinian ideas to the young university liberals of 1867, see Christopher Harvie, *The Lights of Liberalism: University Liberals and the Challenge of Democracy, 1860-1885* (London, 1976), esp. ch. V

[71] e.g. *Essays on Reform*, pp. 1-2, 7, 9 (Brodrick); 274, 278 (Bryce).

for the display of virtue, the proper life of a free man.[72] The casting of a vote was seen as an exercise in moral as well as intellectual self-improvement,[73] and the urban working class was eagerly scrutinized for signs of civic quality· disinterested largeness of view and habits of co-operative action.[74] The urban artisan was, it was urged, more self-respecting and independent than the sycophantic shopkeepers enfranchised by the 1832 Act; master of his trade, he was a free man, mobile and self-reliant—an ironic commercial variant of the old civic republican arguments which had identified independence with a fixed stake in land.[75]

It is tempting, but it would be in important ways misleading, to think of the intellectual liberalism of at least some of the contributions to *Essays on Reform* as a kind of refurbishing of the civic-humanist arguments of the eighteenth century, turned against the cautious accommodations of a Whig establishment on the point of final political dissolution. Certainly the essayists were tinged with republicanism, and certainly, too, the ancient cradle of civic republicanism, Italy, was largely in their thoughts; but the eighteenth century equally certainly was not: it was a classical republicanism mediated by Mazzini rather than the English versions of civic humanism. The essayists' immediate identification was with Young Italy rather than ancient Rome, Garibaldi rather than Brutus or Cato. As with Mazzini's democratic nationalism, their mildly populist and—it is tempting to say—nationalist version of English liberalism contains echoes which are more Christian than classical.[76] We should again beware of making too sharp a contrast between progressive Whig theories of adjustment and the essayists' moralizing. As we have seen in Jeffrey, the two strains often coexisted, if uneasily; the moral quality of

---

[72] Ibid. 274.   [73] Ibid. 66 (Lord Houghton).
[74] Particularly in R. H. Hutton, 'The Political Character of the Working Classes', and Lord Houghton, 'On the Admission of the Working Classes as Part of Our Social System', and in the essay by A. O. Rutson, 'Opportunities and Shortcomings of Government in England' The principled support of Lancashire for the North in the American War, despite its dependence on Southern cotton, and the working-class enthusiasm for Garibaldi were frequently cited examples.
[75] *Essays on Reform*, pp. 27–8, 34–5, 57, 296–7 For 18th-cent. anticipations of this transformation, see Pocock, *Virtue, Commerce and History*, p. 259
[76] e.g. Bryce, 'The Ideal of a Christian State', *Essays on Reform*, p. 274.

the political nation could never be a matter of indifference, even if 'education' came to bulk large in the characterization of it. Full political education demanded participation, and participation both called on, and was, a form of virtue.

Yet there *is* a shift of emphasis, and even—a rather extreme case, admittedly—in Bryce's contribution to *Essays on Reform*, a republican willingness to dabble in notions of a general will, quite alien to the establishment Whig tradition.[77] There was in some sense a bid by these young liberals for the intellectual leadership of the working class, incorporated, through it, into a unified, national community; Thomas Arnold, Mazzini, and Comte are all hovering in the background here.[78] Whig ideas of 'balance' were not just rejected as meaningless—a Benthamite argument Dicey repeated[79]—but found mechanical and amoral. Urban democracy, being an acceptance of the sovereignty of the majority, was necessarily a gamble on widespread virtue or persisting deference, character, or manners, and the essayists were willing to try both. It could not very plausibly be presented as just one more juggle with the representation of interests by the inclusion of yet another, that of the respectable artisans, though until the sweeping nature of the reform actually carried became apparent even this argument still had life in it.[80] What in fact would be counted was numbers. What, in democratic politics, would *count* might perhaps be another matter. The political constitution might be radically simplified, but *society* might—it could be hoped—remain a complex interplay of contending influences.

It is with the perceived implications of all this—often the perception came before the event—and the inherited values

---

[77] Bryce's language here combines something like the Idealist concept of the State soon to be made influential in the work of T H. Green 'the law is the expression of their common will, and their will is to seek not their own good, but the good of all' (p. 274) with an oblique reminiscence of Montesquieu's civic-humanist and sociological dictum that virtue is the principle of republics; Bryce has reminded us earlier (p. 170) that the principle of aristocracies is 'honour'

[78] Harvie stresses their eclecticism, Harvie, *The Lights of Liberalism*, p. 20.

[79] Dicey's essay in *Essays on Reform*, on 'The Balance of Classes', is the most aridly utilitarian and therefore in a sense one of the most 'old-fashioned' of the collection.

[80] Most notably in Houghton's and Stephen's essays.

and conceptual resources that liberal intellectuals brought, often sorrowfully, to their contemplation that we shall chiefly be concerned from now on. What were the prospects for the survival of a Whiggish confidence in the movement of society when that movement led to democracy, and where could that confidence now be placed: in continuing deference to 'enlightened' or 'educated' opinion; in the example of 'character'—the liberal as hero—and its diffusion; or in some modern reformulation of the idea of a balance of countervailing social forces through which liberty and energy might be preserved? We shall be successively concerned with these attempted answers.

# 3
# The Sovereignty of Opinion

WE may begin with a reminder of a concept central to the Scottish Enlightenment which can present itself as a kind of moral paradox: the idea of 'unintended consequences'. It is exemplified for instance, though by no means only there, in Adam Smith's descriptions of the progress of opulence and the natural order of the market. Petty and purely self-interested motives, widely and regularly acted upon, produce far-reaching consequences never envisaged or intended by the great numbers of human agents whose narrow pursuit of their small interests brings them about. An obvious example is Smith's account, in the chapters on the relations of Town and Country in the *Wealth of Nations*,[1] of the origin of commercial society, the parent of modern civility and refinement. With the growth of a money economy, the barons, in commuting services for rent, and preferring to spend their surplus in the market rather than on the maintenance of a large household of retainers, in effect barter their political power for private luxury, and Smith speaks as a stoic moralist in his contempt for the triviality of what they purchase—a few trinkets, a little show and vanity— compared with what they give up. Conversely, the traders and artisans help to bring about a social revolution, the emergence of urban, commercial society, from no higher motive than, as Smith put it, 'their own pedlar principle of turning a penny wherever a penny was to be got'.[2] Yet there is no doubting his approval of the consequences, any more than of their momentousness. The effect is not quite satirical, as it may be in Mandeville's *Fable of the Bees* earlier, with its central violent paradox: private vices are public benefits. Smith is more smoothly ironic: men do better than they know or intend, and

---

[1] Adam Smith, *An Inquiry into the Nature and Causes of the Wealth of Nations* (Oxford University Press, 1976), bk. III, esp. chs. iii and iv
[2] Ibid. 422.

if the ordinary motives of ordinary men produce such consequences, why should we be other than grateful? But Smith's language, like that of other late eighteenth-century Scottish historians of civil society, is not, of course, at all the purged and self-consciously sterilized language of the twentieth-century behavioural scientist, so some elements of the Mandevillian paradox remain, albeit in softened form. Even so it was too much for his friend and admirer Gibbon, himself a greater ironist, but here disturbed that Smith, as he put it, 'proves, perhaps too severely, that the most salutary effects have flowed from the meanest and most selfish causes'[3]

A gap has opened, a certain kind of innocence been lost, and it cannot be closed so long as we retain the knowledge of it. The gap is the disjunction between what men are aware of and intend, and the larger social consequences they unwittingly bring about; and hence also, it may be, a disjunction between what we morally admire and what we sociologically discern, and, as it happens, welcome. The language and stance of the observer are—not occasionally but systematically— no longer the same as those of the participant; there is, so to say, a second order of appraisal which may be different, even in the same writer, from the first-order stance of individual moral choice, approval, and principle.

This is by way of preamble, to be returned to more fully later. With it in mind, we can turn to an example more directly relevant to the question of 'opinion' At the beginning of his essay 'Of the Protestant Succession', Hume imagines for us a Member of Parliament of Anne's reign, weighing the advantages of a Stuart or a Hanoverian succession. He considers the arguments entirely pragmatically, and, in the course of doing so, Hume, or his pragmatic Jacobite persona, draws himself and his readers into a kind of complicity with their less rational selves. It is true, he says, that an anatomist finds no more in a king than in another man, and a moralist perhaps less. Nevertheless, we all have prejudices in favour of birth and family

Or should a man be able, by his superior wisdom, to get entirely above such prepossessions, he would soon *by means of the same*

---

[3] Edward Gibbon, *The History of the Decline and Fall of the Roman Empire*, ed. J. B. Bury, 7 vols. (6th edn., London, 1912), vii. 298 n. 104.

*wisdom*, again bring himself down to them, for the sake of society, whose welfare he would perceive to be intimately connected with them. Far from endeavouring to undeceive the people in this particular, he would cherish such sentiments of reverence to their princes; as requisite to preserve a due subordination in society [4]

The conclusion of Hume's (highly topical) argument does not concern us here. What does, however, is its resolutely utilitarian character (a programme he drily sustains in considering the 'inconvenience' of the Stuarts' Catholic faith), with its implication that the connection between truth and benefit is contingent and variable. Thus, in the *Treatise of Human Nature* we are advised that 'the rigid loyalty to particular persons and families [holds] less of reason than of bigotry and superstition',[5] but also that 'As the slightest properties of the imagination have an effect on the judgements of the people, it shows the wisdom of the laws and of the parliament to take advantage of such properties, and to choose the magistrates either in or out of line, according as the vulgar will most naturally attribute authority and right to them.'[6] A bigoted Jacobitism is unreasonable, but to pay due attention to the preponderant forms of unreason is statesmanlike. Such humouring is made to seem not occasional but intrinsic, by the way custom and imagination work to give the necessary stability to notions of right, even though their origin lies in self-interest.[7]

There are differences between our two examples which we shall have to attend to later, but for the moment we may think of them as illustrations simply of the distance between the perspectives of the observer and the participant, or, in Hume's terms, between the philosopher—the reflective man who temporarily detaches himself from prejudice, in epistemology, morals, and politics, and recognizes its necessary functions—and 'the vulgar' But acceptance of the perennial role of habit, passion, and imagination, as well as interest, in human

---

[4] David Hume, *Essays Moral, Political and Literary* ed. T H. Green and T H. Grose, 2 vols. (London, 1875), I. 472 (emphasis mine). The essay was originally to have appeared in 1748, but its publication was delayed until 1752. Ernest Campbell Mossner, *The Life of David Hume* (2nd edn., Oxford University Press, 1980), 180.
[5] David Hume, *A Treatise of Human Nature*, ed. L. A. Selby-Bigge (Oxford University Press, 1965; 1st edn. 1888), 562.
[6] Ibid. 566. [7] Ibid. 556.

affairs, was a distinctive stance of sceptical Whiggism, which allowed subtle, sometimes even enigmatic, variations in tone and judgement: wry, complacent, grateful, or anxious. In Hume, prejudice is generally seen as making for stability, but the extreme and aggressive divorce of imagination and judgement produces fanaticism or 'enthusiasm', and is to be feared. Moreover— given the initial difficulty, for eighteenth-century minds, of finding in the apparently subjective notions of 'credit' or 'confidence' a basis of stability for commercial society to be compared with the solid independence to be found in real property[8]—to say that 'it is on opinion only that government is founded'[9] may have been to raise possibilities of unease as well as irony [10] And to give opinion this role as the crucial tie between government and governed, as we have seen in Jeffrey, while increasingly dwelling on its historical variability, was to make it a focus for both hope and anxiety His own relation to public opinion, in fact, offered the reflective Whig or liberal a number of possible, and actually more or less successive, roles. There was to be the impresario of Enlightenment, like Jeffrey's mentor Dugald Stewart, or like Macaulay, at his most notorious, banging the drum for the march of mind, or even expertly helping to plan the route;[11] enlightenment was the gift philosophy offered public opinion and the compliment it paid its successful pupil. There was the devout celebrant of the sociological cunning of ancient pieties, like Burke and,

[8] J. G. A. Pocock, *Virtue, Commerce and History: Essays on Political Thought and History Chiefly in the Eighteenth Century* (Cambridge University Press, 1985), 111-13. Pocock sees the conversion of 'credit' into 'opinion' or 'confidence' as the stabilizing of what had been seen as a pathological condition, ibid. 113.

[9] Hume, 'Of the First Principles of Government', in *Essays*, i. 110.

[10] On the potentially disturbing nature of Hume's and Smith's use of opinion, see John Dunn, 'From Applied Theology to Social Analysis; the Break between John Locke and the Scottish Enlightenment', in Istvan Hont and Michael Ignatieff (eds.), *Wealth and Virtue: The Shaping of Political Economy in the Scottish Enlightenment* (Cambridge University Press, 1983), 119-35. Dunn's contrast here is not with civic humanism but with Locke's natural theology

[11] On Stewart, and the contrast between sceptical Whig and prophet of Enlightenment, see Winch in Stefan Collini, Donald Winch, and John Burrow, *That Noble Science of Politics: A Study in Nineteenth-century Intellectual History* (Cambridge University Press, 1983), 42. By comparison with Smith, 'Stewart's notion of progress, by virtue of its emphasis on unilinear intellectual advance, leaves less scope for Nature's deceit or unintended consequences, particularly when dealing with future prospects, and his expectations of the philosopher are, in consequence, more confident, and ambitious'

indeed, Macaulay in another posture.[12] And, by the mid-Victorian years, there was the liberal as historical pessimist — the new part J. S. Mill wrote for him largely out of Tocqueville.

But this is to anticipate. For the moment we are still with the caution of sceptical Whiggism and its conversion into something like an orthodoxy The proof that it took apparently little more than a generation, at most, to render down Hume's paradoxes into Establishment Whig platitudes is Paley's *Principles of Moral and Political Philosophy* Paley's book is in places almost culpably dependent on Hume, yet if there is either irony or anxiety, they are both massively padded with blandness; it became a Cambridge University textbook immediately after its appearance in 1785,[13] and went through sixteen editions by 1806. Paley was the pedagogue's friend. His following of Hume, in his account of the role of opinion in submission to government, is sometimes almost embarrassing. Every government being the rule of the many by the few, we have to ask 'in what manner opinion thus prevails over strength' [14] The lesson for governors is 'that civil authority is founded in opinion; that general opinion therefore ought always to be treated with deference, and managed with delicacy and circumspection' [15] Men are governed partly by individual self-interest, partly by a rational perception of the advantages of government, and partly by prejudice. In dealing with self-interest, it is entirely in keeping with the view we are discussing here that Hume and Paley rejected the 'patriotic' and Country Party political moralism which denounced 'interest' as corruption and the chief threat to constitutional liberty 'Influence', which was the pious constitutionalist's *bête noire*, was to Hume and Paley justified and necessary to prevent the popular element in the constitution, the House of Commons, from becoming all-powerful.[16] It could be seen as another example of 'private vices, public benefits', and Paley's tone in

---

[12] J. W Burrow, *A Liberal Descent: Victorian Historians and the English Past* (Cambridge University Press, 1981), 48, 55, 88–93.

[13] *Dictionary of National Biography*, s.v. 'William Paley'

[14] William Paley, *The Principles of Moral and Political Philosophy*, 2 vols. (16th edn., London, 1806), ii. 131.    [15] Ibid. 136.

[16] Hume, 'Of the Independency of Parliament', in *Essays*, i. 120–1, Paley, *Principles*, ii. 247–9, 250–1. Both make a distinction between influence by honours and preferment and outright bribery

talking of the balance of the constitution, which among radical Whigs and Country Party Tories evoked a cultivated anxiety bordering on hysteria, is, like Blackstone's, blandly confident;[17] it is the tone of the Establishment, utilitarian Whig who can rely confidently on men's small weaknesses, rather than staking all on patriotic virtue. But it is prejudice which is more directly our concern. Prejudice, Paley says, can degenerate into a superstitious support for monarchy, and then, as in 1688, 'breaking the custom' may be beneficial, but in general absurdities and anomalies must often be tolerated. 'Even *names* are not indifferent. When the multitude are to be dealt with, there is a charm in sounds.'[18]

So seen, ruling becomes an exercise in management, and political commentary an appreciation of its conditions, and neither required that one shared the prejudices whose utility one endorsed. It would be crude to speak of this as conspiratorial, just as it was over-simple, if understandable, for his contemporaries to label Hume a Tory Political pragmatism required that each case of the effects of political 'superstition', as both Hume and Paley sometimes called it, was to be considered on its merits; circumstances were crucial and moderation the chief lesson. Popular irrationality might produce faction and tumult as well as acquiescence,[19] while Hume, at least, was sometimes willing to speak ironically of the interests of rulers, as well as of society at large, being served by the sentiment of loyalty 'Education, and the artifice of politicians concur to bestow a further morality on loyalty, and to brand all rebellion with a greater degree of guilt and infamy Nor is it a wonder that politicians should be very industrious in inculcating such notions, where their interest is so particularly concerned.'[20] The destruction of the 'high claims and pretensions' of the Stuarts was plausibly seen as an advantage, even if, for Hume, its long-term consequences were strictly unforeseeable.[21] Hume's reference to the progress of

---

[17] E. N. Williams, *The Eighteenth-Century Constitution, 1688–1815* (Cambridge University Press, 1960), 75.   [18] Paley, *Principles*, ii. 137, 138.
[19] e.g. Hume, 'Of Parties in General', in *Essays*, vol. 1.
[20] *Treatise of Human Nature*, p. 546.
[21] 'Whether the British Monarchy Inclines More to Absolute Monarchy or to a Republic', *Essays*, vol. 1.

enlightenment, at this point, given his avowed preference for a monarchy over a republic, was a somewhat grim compliment:

> there has been a sudden and sensible change in the opinion within these last fifty years, by the progress of learning and liberty Most people, in this island, have divested themselves of all superstitious reverence to names and authority Though the crown, by means of its large revenue, may maintain its authority in times of tranquillity, upon private interest and influence; yet, as the least shock or convulsion must break all these interests to pieces, the royal power being no longer supported by the settled principles and opinions of men, will immediately dissolve.[22]

To refer to possibilities of over-simplification is not, of course, to offer even the most tentative explanatory sketch of what Duncan Forbes has memorably called 'the terrible campaign country' of Hume's political writings, which Forbes himself has done so much to map.[23] I merely want to pave the way for a certain kind of simplicity which now enters the argument, without appearing to endorse its application to Hume. In the later years of the eighteenth century, a deficiency of zeal for enlightenment readily became equated with simple political dishonesty Seen in this way, Paleyan blandness became sinister and Humean scepticism a connivance at convenient imposture. And so, just as in reading Paley one is retrospectively conscious of Hume, so one cannot help being prospectively conscious of Burke's defence of prejudice and custom against the aggressive political rationalism of the revolutionary rights of man. Yet Burke at this point was scarcely bland, nor, except of the arguments of his opponents, exactly a sceptic. What made him so powerful an establishment propagandist, I want to suggest, was that he, outstandingly, was both participant and observer, not simply in the sense that he was an active politician, but in that he could convey the perceptions of a kind of sociology of opinion, founded in sceptical Whiggism, in a language infused with political piety and impassioned commitment. It was a politically necessary modification in the face of accusations of deliberate

---

[22] *Essays*, I. 125.
[23] Duncan Forbes, *Hume's Philosophical Politics* (Cambridge University Press, 1975), p. viii.

mystification and fraud, even if he personally did not escape them. The late eighteenth-century radical Enlightenment, in the writings of Paine, Godwin, Mary Wollstonecraft, the young James Mackintosh, and numerous radical orators, rejected the caution of the Whig establishment, and denounced it as deliberate deceit. The distinction between participant and observer had become a potential source of weakness to the sceptical Whig defender of the established order, because he did not wholly identify with or believe in the prejudice whose value he recognized. It was easy to cry 'fraud'

We have made, in speaking of belief, an important transition. Earlier, in speaking of Smith's conception of unintended consequences, I spoke of a disjunction between intention and result, the moral quality of action and its social consequence. I then went on to speak of an analogous, but not identical, disjunction, in the case of Hume and Paley, between the *truth* of a *belief* and its social consequences. That there is an analogy is clear. The stance in both cases—towards motive and towards belief—is one it seems proper to call ironic. Private follies, as well as private vices, may be public benefits. But though there is an analogy, there are also significant differences—founded on the difference between motive in the one case, belief in the other—in the nature of the arguments developed later to support the one position and the other We shall have to turn to those differences in a moment, but we need first to consider more generally the question of an ironic attitude towards other people's beliefs and their social consequences. The most obvious case, of course, is religion, and in speaking of religion we are not at all turning away from the preoccupations of the late eighteenth-century Enlightenment, either in its Establishment Whig or in its radical and revolutionary aspects. For the Paineite radical or Jacobin of the 1790s, Church and King are two faces of the same idol, and, given a more reverent terminology, Burke would have agreed.

The disjunction, in the account of religion, between belief and social endorsement is essentially the classical doctrine of the 'double truth' It is a characteristic one among thinkers of the Enlightenment, as also is its radical critical counterpart, the conspiracy theory of religion. The best-known example of the former is Gibbon's sympathetic portrait of the Roman aristocrat in the age of the Antonines, performing his religious duties as a social obligation, 'viewing with a smile of pity and indulgence the various errors of the vulgar', and concealing 'the sentiments of an atheist under the sacerdotal robes'[24] In Paris Gibbon was shocked by the intolerant atheistic zeal of the circle of Helvétius and d'Holbach, and Hume seems to have felt much the same.[25] The hostile critical version of the double truth, current in France, was the diagnosis of religion as a deliberate conspiracy for the maintenance of priestly and political authority, as it can be seen, for example, in Condorcet's *Sketch of the Progress of the Human Mind*. A priestly caste monopolizes knowledge, including knowledge of the workings of the natural world, and uses its knowledge to overawe and rule the multitude. Power is rooted in mystification; the progress of enlightenment, the advance and diffusion of genuine knowledge and philosophy, is also the progress of emancipation from superstition and unaccountable authority ruling in its own interest.[26]

It is here that the distinction I drew a moment ago becomes relevant. For between Smith's moral disjunction, in the *Wealth of Nations*, and Gibbon's double truth there seems to be also an important difference. It is one which makes Gibbon's position vulnerable, in a way Smith's in the economic sphere is not, and it is the matter of rationality Smith may not have to admire the petty avarice of his artisan or shopkeeper, but he cannot and does not wish to *refute* it. Refutation is not relevant to motive, only to belief, and in any case, the pedlar principle of buying in the cheapest market and selling in the dearest, far from being irrational, seems to be a paradigm case of rational behaviour. In fact this is an over-simplification of Smith: in his austere view our real wants are easily satisfied, and the motive of most economic striving is vanity[27] But this is a qualification which does not essentially affect our argument. The differences between the kinds of opposition which emerged

---

[24] Gibbon, *Decline and Fall*, 1. 30–1.
[25] Patricia B. Craddock, *Young Edward Gibbon, Gentleman of Letters* (Baltimore, 1982), 169 Cf. Mossner, *Life of Hume*, pp. 485–6.
[26] F M. de Condorcet, *Sketch for an Historical Picture of the Progress of the Human Mind* (1794–5; English trans., J. Barraclough, London, 1955).
[27] See above, ch. 2 n. 25.

later, opposition to the disjunction of motive from consequence in social and economic life, and of belief from consequence in religion and also political life—we shall have to come back to the connection with politics in a moment—bear out the point that there is indeed a crucial difference.

We can see this most clearly in the early nineteenth century by considering the reception of Malthus.[28] The most enthusiastic proponents of the Malthusian doctrine of population were the Philosophical Radicals, the heirs of the Enlightenment. It is true that Malthus had originally been provoked to formulate his theory by what seemed the facile utopianism of Condorcet and Godwin, who were themselves ardent spokesmen of a radical Enlightenment. But by the early nineteenth century in England, the Enlightenment, in the more hard-headed form of Philosophic Radicalism, had shed sentimental utopianism. In what became the test case, for the period, of the doctrine of unintended consequences, the Malthusian theory of population, the battle lines were on the whole simple. Malthus's defenders belonged to the tradition of the Enlightenment; his chief detractors were its opponents, the Romantics and traditionalists and advocates of a patriarchal social order: Southey, Coleridge, Cobbett, Carlyle. In rejecting Political Economy they rejected the concept of unintended consequences, and called instead for spiritual regeneration and the restoration of the integrity of moral and economic life, by applying moral precepts, charity, and brotherhood directly to economic policy One test case was the Factory Acts, but the more general issue was Malthusian theory and the new poor-law For Malthus, though this was certainly not his own view, seemed to many of his contemporaries to have made—more harshly than Smith, more practically than Mandeville—private virtue apparently pernicious and vice a source of benefit. For in Malthus's theory, sexual vice, though of course he did not advocate it, acts as one of the checks on over-population, while early marriage promotes it. It is not the strange woman who waits by the gate, but the little woman who waits on the hearth who embodies the chief threat to human felicity It is not

---

[28] e.g. H. A. Boner, *Hungry Generations: The Nineteenth-century Case against Malthusianism* (London, 1955).

surprising that Malthus, however unfairly, had to endure the accusation of having slandered virtue and recommended vice. In embracing Political Economy and defending Malthus, the Philosophic Radicals accepted the doctrine of unintended consequences in economic life as one of their chief defining characteristics, and so won a large part of their reputation for being harsh, unfeeling, and coldly mechanical.

In religion and politics, on the other hand, the reverse is the case; Enlightenment in all its radical forms, utopian or utilitarian, seems, so to speak, to wear out its patience with the double truth; Voltairean and Gibbonian irony increasingly give way to Godwinian or Benthamite demands for openness, simplicity, and truth. So far, then, the distinction we saw turning on the rationality of economic action and the irrationality of religious belief seems vindicated. For in Gibbon's stance we have not just distance but social hauteur, not simply the detachment of the philosopher but the conspiratorial knowingness of an élite. The relation postulated between the wise few and the prejudiced many is, after all, uncomfortably close to what eighteenth-century writers, including Gibbon, often identified and denounced as the connection between the power of the despot and the ignorance and intellectual degradation of his subjects—that alliance of servility and superstition which, in the *Decline and Fall*, is epitomized in Byzantium. And indeed, there is a real distinction here. The Political Economist can bear the charge of hard-heartedness because he can assert that economic activity, if not lovable or beautiful, is rational as well as beneficial. The advocate, or something like it, of the religious or political double truth will find it hard to rebut charges of fraud, because he knows there is something in them. He will need a subtler, a more rhetorically seductive, and, best of all, perhaps, a more heartfelt type of defence, and that is what Burke provided.

But to remind ourselves why it was needed we have to return again to the critics and accusers, and to a rough but usable distinction between an earlier, sceptical phase of the eighteenth-century Enlightenment, which easily accommodated the doctrine of unintended consequences, the idea of the double truth, and a confident, Paleyan, Establishment Whiggism, and a late eighteenth-century radical, democratic Enlightenment whose spokesmen are Condorcet and Paine and Godwin. In France, in Condorcet and others, it produced a conspiracy theory of religion and politics. In England, an equivalent confidence in the march of the mind as the central fact of contemporary history, providing illimitable hopes for the future, was combined with a native tradition of religious dissent. Many of the radicals of the period were Dissenters; Paine was of Quaker stock, Godwin had been a Sandemanian. All this combined to produce a denunciation of civil and religious establishments, and an apocalyptic vision of a restored transparency and simplicity in human relations, in which it is often difficult to disentangle the inherited Puritanism from the Enlightenment rationalism and the Rousseauist cult of simplicity Paine speaks in the accents of sixteenth- and seventeenth-century Protestantism when he says:

> It is not among the least of the evils of the present existing governments in all parts of Europe, that man, considered as man, is thrown back to a vast distance from his Maker, and the artificial chasm filled up by a succession of barriers, or a sort of turnpike gates, through which he has to pass. I will quote Mr Burke's catalogue of barriers that he has set up between man and his Maker. Putting himself in the character of a herald he says—'We fear God—we look with awe to kings—with affection to parliaments—with duty to magistrates—with reverence to priests, and with respect to nobility' Mr Burke has forgotten to put in *chivalry*. He has also forgotten to put in Peter.[29]

Not all radicals spoke in this way Notable exceptions are the Scottish radical Whigs, John Millar, and, still more at this point, in the early 1790s, the young James Mackintosh. They spoke a language without religious resonance and located the progress of 'Philosophy', in characteristically Scottish fashion, in a context of social change. As Mackintosh said in *Vindiciae Galliae*, attacking Burke's famous and already notorious evocation of chivalry· 'Commerce and diffused knowledge have, in fact, so completely assumed the ascendant in polished nations, that it will be difficult to discover any relics of Gothic manners, but in a fantastic exterior, which has survived the

---

[29] Thomas Paine, *The Rights of Man*, in *The Complete Writings of Thomas Paine*, 2 vols. (New York, 1969), I. 275.

generous illusions which made these manners splendid and seductive.'³⁰ The contrast of modern and archaic, interior and exterior, meant that Burke was either the victim of anachronistic illusion or an accomplice of political fraud. Mackintosh said that in Burke's *Reflections*

> The expediency of *political imposture* is the whole force of the argument. To pronounce that men are only to be governed by delusion is to libel the human understanding, and to consecrate the frauds that have elevated Despots and Muftis, Pontiffs and Sultans, on the ruin of degraded and oppressed humanity But the doctrine is as false as it is odious. Primary political truths are few and simple. It is easy to make them understood, and to transfer to Government the same enlightened self-interest that presides in the other concerns of life.³¹

The rhetoric here seems to attempt to rival his opponent's, but the central thought is one we are accustomed to hearing more flatly or wryly expressed by his other great contemporary, Bentham: a bid, in politics, for the sovereignty of enlightened self-interest, unaided or tainted by prejudice and custom. Mackintosh's fellow-Scot and radical Whig, John Millar, suited manner to matter and spoke the language of utility unadorned, though he also invoked natural rights. In his *Historical View of the English Government* Millar assumed the historian's privilege of speaking of the transition he favoured, from prejudice to perceived utility, as one already virtually completed:

> The mysteries of government have been more and more unveiled The blind respect and reverence paid to ancient institutions has given place to a desire of examining their uses, of criticising their defects, and of appreciating their true merits. The fashion of scrutinising public measures by the standard of their utility has now become very universal.³²

Millar is a complex political and social thinker· utilitarian, Country Whig, Foxite, and late representative of the Scottish

---

³⁰ James Mackintosh, *Vindiciae Galliae* (2nd edn., London, 1791), 198.
³¹ Ibid. 307–8.
³² *An Historical View of the English Government from the Settlement of the Saxons in Britain to the Revolution of 1688*, 4 vols. (London, 1812), iii. 305.

## The Sovereignty of Opinion

Enlightenment;³³ capable of making at least a retrospective pragmatic case for the double truth in the case of 'the great body of the people' 'Those feelings of the human mind which give rise to authority may be regarded as the wise provision of nature for supporting the order and government of society '³⁴

When the English radicals in the Dissenting tradition exposed sham and imposture, by contrast, the rhetoric of Puritan simplicity and zeal-for-truth is seldom far off. The victory of Philosophy over Prejudice and Illusion (it seems travesty to go into the pinched modernity of the lower case) becomes eschatological. We see it, for example, in Letitia Barbauld's elegant apocalypse, in 1790·

> The genius of Philosophy is walking abroad, and with the touch of Ithuriel's spear is trying the establishments of the earth. The various forms of Prejudice, Superstition and Servility start up in their true shapes, which had so long imposed upon the world under the revered semblances of Honour, Faith and Loyalty Whatever is loose must be shaken, whatever is corrupted must be lopt away; whatever is not built on the broad basis of public utility must be thrown to the ground.³⁵

We see the stripping, simplifying, Puritan mentality again, the craving for directness and transparency of relations, modestly expressed in Mary Wollstonecraft's denunciation of the artificiality of relations between the sexes and of women's acceptance of their merely external, decorative role. The revolutionary debate became a kind of contest of sincerity, in which, at least until the more bizarre rituals of the Revolution were unveiled (out of which Burke made capital), the

---

[33] Michael Ignatieff, 'John Millar and Individualism' in Hont and Ignatieff, *Wealth and Virtue*, pp. 317-43.

[34] Millar, *Historical View of the English Government*, iii. 310. Millar follows Hume and Smith on what those feelings are and why we have them, ibid. 288, 290-1. It is easy to make the lines of division between scepticism and 'enlightenment' too sharp, and we can match this concession by Millar with Burke's declaration in 1778 that 'Too little dependence [the sense requires 'much'] cannot be had, at this time of day, on names and prejudices. The eyes of mankind are opened, and communities must be held together by an evident solid interest.' 'Two Letters to Gentlemen in Bristol', in *The Writings and Speeches of Edmund Burke*, 12 vols. (London, 1900), ii. 251.

[35] Quoted in Alfred Cobban (ed.), *The Debate on the French Revolution 1789-1800* (London, 1950), 49-50.

accusers had the initial advantage. Constant resort was made to the imagery of the theatre, as well as to that of idolatry Mary Wollstonecraft used both when, referring to Burke's notorious lament for Marie Antoinette, she spoke of 'the declamations of the theatre' and 'the anguish that rent your heart when the gorgeous robes were torn off the idol human weakness had set up' [36] Mackintosh spoke of 'the stage trick of Royalty',[37] and Paine of 'the puppet-show of state and aristocracy', and said he could not think of Burke's *Reflections* 'in any other light than a dramatic performance' [38] Where Burke had spoken of 'the decent drapery of life', Mary Wollstonecraft saw 'the idle tapestry that decorated a Gothic pile' [39] We find the Puritan contempt for public symbolism most effectively, because most earthily, expressed in Paine, as in his famous remark that the crown in which power is said to reside is 'a metaphor, shown at the Tower for sixpence or a shilling a-piece' [40]

In a contest of sincerity, of course, the advocate of the double truth has no chance; nor has the sceptic in a contest of zeal. It is a self-contradiction to imagine a sceptical Whig martyr. Yet Burke was a man of whom it is not absurd to imagine martyrdom; he was, as it were, an enthusiast against enthusiasm. But this is to misuse the eighteenth-century terminology; Burke's arguments, in eighteenth-century terms, had more to do with enthusiasm's antithesis, superstition.[41] Hume had given the classic account of the distinction, in constructing his profiles of the two types of irrationality In his essay 'Of Superstition and Enthusiasm', we see both the Enlightenment's fascination with the origin of religion, and also the Augustan distaste for 'enthusiasm', in which historical memories of the godly zeal of the seventeenth-century sectaries still rankled. Superstition was despised, but enthusiasm was

---

[36] Cobban, *Debate on the French Revolution*, 83, 85.
[37] Mackintosh, *Vindiciae Galliae*, p. 20.
[38] Paine, *The Rights of Man*, in *Complete Writings*, i. 267-8.
[39] Cobban, op. cit., 84.
[40] Paine, *The Rights of Man*, in *Complete Writings*, i. 283.
[41] Burke himself employed the distinction; e.g. arguing for the possible social benefits of monastic institutions, he admitted that they 'savour of superstition' and 'are the products of enthusiasm', but added characteristically, 'they are the *instruments* of wisdom' (emphasis mine), *Reflections on the Revolution in France*, in *Writings and Speeches*, iii. 442, 441.

to be feared. Superstition, in Hume's account, comes from timidity, from the desire to propitiate. Enthusiasm, however, is bold: an utter belief in the infallibility of one's own private judgement. Hence, superstition supports establishments, enthusiasm overthrows them.[42]

Gibbon, of course, knew Hume's categories and often seems to apply them in the *Decline and Fall*. Faced with the choice, he more readily pardoned superstition, especially when the Establishment was pagan, while Christian iconoclastic enthusiasm he saw with extreme distaste (only in the case of Byzantium, for him the nadir of superstition, did he show a Protestant sympathy with iconoclasm).[43] In identifying the French Revolution as a new outbreak of enthusiasm, he naturally made his usual choice, and hailed Burke as a champion: 'I approve his politics, I adore his chivalry, and I can even forgive his superstition.' All the equivocation we have been considering is in that 'even' [44]

But diagnosis is not rebuttal, and antinomian utopianism *is* hard to answer. The answer involves defending complexity—always a hard thing to do—and endorsing role-playing, compromises, half-measures, half-truths, in a way that seems mean-spirited. It calls for a defence of Burke's 'riches of convention' in a fashion inevitably apparently compromised, in anyone not actually an anchorite, by complicity and self-interest (it is usual at this point to forget that the *argumentum ad hominem* is a fallacy). Yet though Burke's vehemence and exaggeration were sometimes an embarrassment to later, less embattled and fearful generations, it was surely important to the Establishment Whigs' position that Burke was able to meet the radicals with a passion and conviction equal to their own, and with the rhetorical resources to make the moral case for complexity Burke seemed, in his passion, his combination of piety and sociological awareness, to have resolved a moral dilemma created by the doctrine of unintended consequences

---

[42] Hume, 'Of Superstition and Enthusiasm', in *Essays*, I. 144-50.
[43] J. W Burrow, *Gibbon* (Oxford University Press, 1985), 52-5, 63-6. For a more wide-ranging discussion, see Pocock, 'Gibbon's *Decline and Fall* and the World View of the Late Enlightenment', in *Virtue, Commerce and History*, pp. 143-56.
[44] *The Letters of Edward Gibbon*, ed. J. E. Norton, 3 vols. (London, 1956), iii. 216.

in politics and the disjunction of utility and belief. He, supremely, was able to combine the first-order language of commitment and belief with the sceptical Whig's perception of the utility of the irrational. A providential view of history could moralize unintended consequences, and Burke's references to the complex interaction of diverse social interests, 'various multiform and intricate',[45] have none of the irony which marked Smith's, despite the latter's invocation of the unseen hand. Burke's celebration of unplanned, complex social harmonies was another version of the concept of unintended consequences, seen, not ironically but with pious and appreciative wonder, as though by a natural theologian contemplating the providentially arranged integration and prodigal inventiveness of nature. Social life was an infinitely complicated tissue of habits, affections, allegiances, and inhibitions, of various kinds and intensities, mostly not brought fully to consciousness.

But Burke's was a holding operation. It was through the intellectual resources of the Scottish tradition of the history of civil society that, under the intellectual leadership of the *Edinburgh Review*, pragmatic Whiggism acquired a creed which made for confidence in modernity and a sense of mission to enlighten, without any of the apocalyptic expectations of the 1790s. In fact, if we map a kind of trajectory of opinions of 'opinion' from sceptical or philosophical Whigs to educated Liberals (the change of characteristic adjective has its own story), from Hume to J. S. Mill, then the period when the *Edinburgh Review* became itself a powerful organ of opinion seems, perhaps partly for that reason, a high-water mark of optimism.[46] It is true that among the radical Whigs of the 1780s and early 1790s confidence in the social capacity of enlightened or philosophical opinion was even higher, but, as we have seen, it tended to transcend the sociological relativism of 'opinion' for the absolute of 'truth'. But even for those with soberer expectations, when the most urgent political task seemed to be to curtail the influence of patronage, it was easy and tactically sound to emphasize the virtues of public opinion.

---

[45] See above, ch. 2 n. 37
[46] But see Winch on Jeffrey's reservations, in Collini, Winch, and Burrow, *That Noble Science*, p. 55.

But there was a balance to be held, because the threat to orderly progress was represented by radical impatience and an excess of rationalism as well as by a constitution in some respects archaic. A characteristic tone of the *Edinburgh Review* was an exasperated common sense, and the common sense was as important as the exasperation. We see the blend of elements such a Whiggism required most perfectly articulated in Macaulay Macaulay notoriously enjoyed an exhilarating sense of confidence and even jubilation in the progress of civil society But he was heir to other intellectual traditions as well: to the Foxite constitutionalist pieties of Holland House,[47] and to a Burkian awareness of the utility of prejudice, which did not exclude large possibilities of complicity They combined in him with a seductiveness equal to Burke's, uniting a genuine, first-order attachment to the pieties of the English Whig tradition, as he interpreted it, with a second-order perception of their utility It was a perception grounded, like Hume's and Smith's analysis of prejudice, in the eighteenth-century tradition of association psychology·

there is often a portion of willing credulity and enthusiasm in the veneration which the most discerning men pay to their political idols. From the very nature of man it must be so. The faculty by which we inseparably associate ideas which have often been presented to us in conjunction is not under the absolute control of the will.[48]

This is then made, in entirely eighteenth-century fashion, into a distinction between the philosophical view of what Macaulay, ironically pressing the religious analogy, calls 'the initiated', and that of 'the vulgar' 'Every political sect has its esoteric and its exoteric school, its abstract doctrines for the initiated, its visible symbols, its imposing, its theological fables for the vulgar It assists the devotion of those who are unable to raise themselves to the contemplation of pure truth '[49] The fundamental thought is Humean, but the language is already, prospectively, the language of Bagehot's *The English Constitution*—and we know that Bagehot was an ardent reader

---

[47] Leslie Mitchell, *Holland House* (London, 1980), ch. 2.
[48] 'Hallam's History of England', in *The Works of Lord Macaulay*, ed. Lady Trevelyan, 8 vols. (London, 1897), v 165.
[49] Ibid. 164–5.

of Macaulay's essays.[50] But there are two additionally noteworthy features in Macaulay's self-consciousness about political piety One is that, unlike Bagehot, but like Burke, he includes himself among the devout as well as, necessarily, among the philosophers. Even the most discerning are not exempt from enthusiasm and willing credulity It is this which explains the vast difference in tone between Macaulay's *History* and Bagehot's *English Constitution*. The second is that Macaulay's irony in the essay on Hallam is exercised at the expense of the symbols of party When it came to those which could be thought of as belonging to the historic nation itself (even if Britain, in Macaulay's hands, became a somewhat Whiggish entity), irony was generally muted. Even the fierce Protestant symbolism and rituals of Ulster evoked, with misgiving, an unsceptical, uncondescending response: 'it is impossible not to respect the sentiment which expresses itself by these tokens. It is a sentiment which belongs to the higher and purer part of human nature '[51] It is easy to imagine Burke writing that, though perhaps not of the same manifestations; impossible to imagine it said by Hume or Bagehot.

Macaulay and Bagehot are the most obvious and distinguished successors to Burke; without making too much of differences which were at least in part temperamental, it is possible to see them as marking successive stages of an increasing — and increasingly awkward — sociological detachment, in ways which express more general changes in political circumstances and culture. There are at times elements of detachment and irony in Macaulay's handling of the heritage of Whig constitutionalism, in its broadest sense,[52] yet his relation to those who exemplified it in the past is still on the whole that of an accomplice. In Bagehot's impatience with 'historic twaddle about the rise of British liberty',[53] and his ironies at the expense of constitutionalist pieties generally, the rift between first-order commitment and

---

[50] R. H. Hutton, 'Walter Bagehot', *Fortnightly Review*, 22 (1877), 456.
[51] Macaulay, *Works*, ii. 585.
[52] See Burrow, *A Liberal Descent*, pp. 51-2.
[53] 'Responsible Government', in *The Collected Works of Walter Bagehot*, ed. Norman St John-Stevas, 15 vols. (London, 1965-86), vi. 99

second-order appraisal, between the initiated and the vulgar, is stark.[54]

'Should a man be able, by his superior wisdom, to get entirely above such prepossessions, he would soon by reason of the same wisdom, again bring himself down to them.'[55] Bagehot saw no need for the personal sacrifice of superiority, and, in fact, constructed his literary personality out of refusing to make it, while he pointed, in endless variations, to the element of wisdom in the prescription. There is much in Bagehot to remind us of Hume; much more than there is of Burke.[56] But there was also a liberal impatience; Bagehot was fascinated by the compromises of political and public life, to the extent of finding his *métier* in ironic analysis of them, but there was also a side of him that found them tragic.[57] Inside Bagehot's ironist there was a restless managerial progressive trying to get out, and his impatience was touched by the vocabulary of Romanticism and by scorn for the middle classes; the largest gulf in Bagehot is not just between philosophy and prejudice, but between 'the man of genius' and 'the obstinacy of stupidity',[58] with the limited, practical reformer, the archetypal Whig, as mediator.[59]

The concept of progress was crucial, and even in his recognitions of its slow, laborious course, and attendant compromises, Bagehot paid his tribute to it: 'The man of genius is an age or two in advance.'[60] Meanwhile, established institutions and the prejudices attached to them might be an incubator rather than an obstacle. The Paineite revolutionary's contrast between inside and outside, reality and sham (the 'theatrical'[61] parts of

---

[54] This argument is a necessarily much-compressed version of an earlier attempt to examine the notion of Bagehot as belonging to a Burkian tradition of thought. For the fuller version see 'Sense and Circumstances: Bagehot and the Nature of Political Understanding', in Collini, Winch, and Burrow, *That Noble Science*, pp. 161–81.
[55] Hume, above, pp. 51–2.
[56] Bagehot clearly knew Hume's and Smith's writings well, and admired the latter in particular, though it is surprising that he thought little of *The Theory of Moral Sentiments* (Bagehot, 'Adam Smith as Person', in *Works*, iii. 95); Smith, there, and Hume, in 'Of National Characters' (and elsewhere), dealt with questions always of central concern to Bagehot, above all what Hume called 'sympathy or contagion of manners', *Essays*, i. 249 Cf. Bagehot, *Physics and Politics* (London, 1869), ch. 3.
[57] e.g. 'The Character of Sir Robert Peel', in *Works*, v 245.
[58] 'Average Government', in *Works*, vi. 88.
[59] e.g. *Works*, i. 318–19     [60] *Works*, vi. 88.
[61] *The English Constitution*, in *Works*, v 209

the constitution whose function is to excite reverence) allowed an optimistic, and hence gradualist, and Whiggish, if somewhat conspiratorial, interpretation: 'it is needful to keep the ancient show while we secretly interpolate the new reality.'[62]

The concept of progress was crucial here, and it was a good deal more schematic in Bagehot's view of history, in the manner of his period, than in Hume or Smith. In fact, we can speak more widely than just of the interpretation of Bagehot in saying that the idea of progress, both as the overall direction of historical movement and as the pressure imparted to it by the statesman and reflective journalist, gave respectability to notions of adjustment to, or management of, public opinion. The nineteenth-century Whig, rejecting the utilitarian claim that enlightened self-interest alone is a sufficient support for social order, necessarily also rejected Bentham's hostility to 'fictions', to symbolism and rhetorical uses of language,[63] and involved himself in a compromising and pliable relation to a fluctuating and sometimes not altogether reputable entity, 'the state of opinion.' In fact, as the historic, Foxite, elements in the Whig creed, above all suspicion of the influence of the monarchy, became increasingly irrelevant, its relation to public opinion came to constitute the Whig Party's *raison d'être*. As one of its historians has said, 'There was no prevalent desire to go faster than "public opinion" required; they deemed it no presumption that their politicians should be the judge of this, and for "public opinion" they read "political expediency".'[64] The reforming Whig's stance and confidence, in the early years of the century, had been justified by the claim to sense the long-term movement of society, and to know that it was on the whole beneficial; later, when the intellectual capital (much of it Scottish) accumulated during the years of opposition had been expended in the reforming legislation of the 1830s (or filched by the Tories), it became plausible to speak of the Whigs as a party without principle. Yet it could be said that the management of consensus *was* its principle; one with which

---

[62] *The English Constitution*, in *Works*, v. 392.

[63] I use the Benthamite example here, rather than the ones we considered earlier (above, pp. 62–4), because Benthamism became, in the nineteenth century, the most intellectually formidable version of this kind of reductionist radical argument.

[64] Donald Southgate, *The Passing of the Whigs 1832–1886* (London, 1962), 78.

zealous and radical spirits were naturally impatient. Tories, Radicals, and advanced liberals alike could agree on the Whigs' chameleon character.

Complaints that politicians were the puppets of public opinion became something of a cliché; it was a hostile way of putting what was often, of course, spoken of with approval, or at least resignation: the long-term predominance of the energies of society over political forms and theories. 'The statesman is to follow, not to lead—to study tastes rather than carry out principles. A pointer-like faculty of seeing the direction which the game is taking, under the name of a clear perception of the signs of the times, is the most enviable of his gifts.'[65] This was the pejorative view, ironically put, but the concept of progress could offer redemption. In so far as public opinion was thought of as merely fickle and directionless, it was hard to escape charges that indulgence to its prejudices and exploitation of its foibles was mere cynicism and time-serving. But progress came to the rescue in one of two ways. Either public opinion was not merely directionless, but an aspect of a progressively developing society, in which case to receive its promptings was time-serving only in the entirely respectable sense of feeling the pulse of the great movement; the statesman and intellectual could find roles in terms of, as J. S. Mill put it, 'what great improvement stands next in order'[66] Or the balance could be tilted somewhat, within the same fundamental way of thinking, to make it less determinate and more flexible: the politician or author becomes guide rather than receiver, with a responsibility to his vision of what Mill called 'a certain order of *possible* progress'[67] (emphasis mine); the degree of historical determinism reached is not always easy to judge, and can shift from phrase to phrase. Tactful management of one's contemporaries might involve large, but, one might hope, only temporary, concessions to their intellectual vices; the distance between what was perceived as true and what was seen as sociologically functional might be made morally innocuous given sufficient confidence in the long run.

---

[65] George Brodrick, *Political Studies* (London, 1879), 137 Cf. above, ch. 2 n. 8.
[66] J. S. Mill, *Autobiography* ed. J. Stillinger (Oxford University Press, 1971), 102.) [67] Ibid. 97

The idea of progress had many functions in nineteenth-century politics and intellectual life, and one of them was to introduce an element of principled conviction or conscious education into the intellectual Whig's and Liberal's conception of free government as necessarily concerned with the sensitive reception and delicate management of public opinion.[68] The notion of the role of the statesman and political commentator as educative provided a way, for those who needed it, of reconciling a principled liberal concern for truth with sociological sophistication about the possible utility of habit and even error. Often the difference between the advanced liberal rationalist and the belated sceptical Whig turns out to be a question of timing. The former, of whom Herbert Spencer would be the extreme case, tended to reserve his sociology for the past—prejudice and custom had been useful once—and to speak like a radical impatient for the simplification and transparency of social relations in the present and immediate future.[69] Bagehot, on the other hand, alternated between free use of the principle of unripe time and an apparent belief that custom and prejudice, in various forms, would always provide the necessary ballast for an ordered social life. The relation between progressive ideas, the animating principle in society, and a sluggish yet stabilizing public opinion was the continuous preoccupation of Bagehot's life, indulged to repetitiousness. We do not usually bracket the two names together, yet much the same, if we omit the reference to 'stabilizing', could be said of J. S. Mill. For both of them—and not only for them, of course, among mid-Victorian liberals—to consider the relation between original ideas, the discovery of truth, and public opinion, ideally harmonized in the notion of an orderly, non-revolutionary progress, was to identify their own role: the role of the intellectual as persuader, simultaneously committed to truth and the effective exercise of influence. Of course, their view of the role was differently accented; Bagehot believed in truth, but he was fascinated by the conditions of political effectiveness. Mill avoided a dilemma by arguing—and here

---

[68] 'The condition of a free government is that you must persuade the present generation', Bagehot, 'Average Government', in *Works*, vi. 88.
[69] Burrow, *Evolution and Society* (Cambridge University Press, 1966), 226-7

at least he spoke in the line of his Philosophic Radical heritage—that the proclamation of the truth (he would add the un-Benthamite rider 'as one saw it') was the supreme exercise of one's social responsibility; truth was always in the long run useful.[70] Bagehot was interested in coaxing, Mill in testifying, and if the former admired the effectiveness of the *Edinburgh* Reviewers, the latter was influenced, in his conception of the intellectual and of the free market in ideas, not only by an inherited Puritan dislike of establishments, but also, in later years, with a *frisson* of unease, by the Comtist conception of the priesthood of science, handing down truth with the force of authority and reinforcing its dictates by ersatz religious rituals.

There was at least one contemporary attempt to adjudicate between Bagehot on the utility of the double truth and the defiant testifying acclaimed in Mill's *On Liberty*, though it did not invoke the two names. John Morley understood very well, and deplored, the transition from first-order moral judgement to the spectatorial appraisal suggested by constant reference to the state of public opinion. As he said, 'Opinions are counted rather as phenomena to be explained than as matters of truth and falsehood.'[71] Morley's argument here was an aspect of that unease with what was often felt as the fatalistic as well as relativistic implications of the historical and sociological points of view we considered earlier, and it was seen as distinctively modern: 'In the last century men asked of a belief or story, Is it true? We now ask, How did men come to take it for true?'[72]

Morley, like Bagehot, was preoccupied with the influencing of opinion, though as a disciple of Comte and J. S. Mill.[73] His books on Turgot, Condorcet, and Burke were studies of intellectuals in politics. He was, again like Bagehot, a successful editor,[74] but he also achieved the political career Bagehot

[70] J. S. Mill, *On Liberty* (1859), in *The Collected Works of John Stuart Mill*, ed. J. M. Robson (Toronto, 1977), vol. iii, ch. 2.
[71] John Morley, *On Compromise* (London, 1886; 1901 edn.), 30.
[72] Ibid. 31. Morley here attributed the blame to 'The Historic Method'
[73] I am indebted to the very acute discussion of Morley in Christopher Kent, *Brains and Numbers: Elitism, Comtism and Democracy in Mid-Victorian England* (Toronto, 1978), 107-33.
[74] Of the *Fortnightly Review* and then of the *Pall Mall Gazette*.

had yearned for (a long career, ended on a point of principle, when he resigned from the Cabinet over the entry of Britain into the war in 1914). In the year *On Compromise* was published he became Chief Secretary for Ireland. Yet, by comparison with Bagehot, *On Compromise* is a very unworldly book, with none of the former's felicity in distinguishing and illustrating the modes of political and intellectual influence. Morley, in raising—and, with only marginal reservations, rejecting—the idea of the double truth, chose instead to preach a sermon on intellectual integrity and the necessity for 'character.' Morley writes as a moralist, a child of Puritanism and a disciple of Mill. His chief concession really lay in the notion that such a book was worth writing, that there was something to discuss. He is strongly critical of Bagehot's kind of cynicism—the name is not mentioned but seems fairly clearly intended—in its view of the utility of shams.[75] But to turn from Bagehot's ironic pragmatism to Morley's casuistry for intellectuals in politics is to feel that the point of a century of sometimes uneasy political sophistication, from Hume and Paley to Macaulay and Bagehot, has been missed rather than addressed. The result, reiteration that honesty is the best policy, was a high-mindedness which, with small empirical content and resting on little more than simple faith, did not bode well for the fate of Morley's kind of liberalism in the emerging conditions of democratic mass politics.[76] To take the story further would be to consider the role of the intellectual in that politics, and to look, most obviously, at Graham Wallas's *Human Nature in Politics* (1908), his classic and dismayed study of the manipulation of mass electorates by political techniques pioneered initially in commercial advertising. And though the vanity of consumers and their associative habits of mind, on which that advertising depended, would have held no surprises for any reader of Smith's *Theory of Moral Sentiments*, we should have travelled, ostensibly at least, a long way from Hume and Paley on custom and prejudice as guarantees of stability

---

[75] *On Compromise*, 224.
[76] Though Morley, as the future biographer of Gladstone, could have found more complex lessons in his hero.

Too far, indeed, for a single lecture, and we can leave the liberals of the 1860s and 1870s with their forebodings. To Mill, and Morley, the polarity we have considered, between the intellectual's responsibility to truth and progress, and the public opinion on which he works, was always the subject of their most anxious contemplation; it gave them their sense of purpose and identity, as it did, in a more relaxed way, to Bagehot also. But to say 'on which he works' is to speak optimistically, to think in terms, in Bagehot's phrase, 'of the daily play of the higher mind upon the lower',[77] which, differently phrased, was like James Mill's account of the salutary political influence of the middle classes on their inferiors.[78] In the middle years of the nineteenth century we find something it seems fair to call a loss of confidence in the march of mind, a sense that the man of intellect may be not so much the educator of society as its victim. The pressure of uneducated or half-educated opinion, of conventional ideas and narrow, torpid minds, is felt as oppressive and seen as ominous. Bagehot, who always saw the British public as irritatingly if reassuringly bovine (the French were another matter), said, 'public opinion is a permeating influence, and it exacts obedience to itself; it requires us to think other men's thoughts, to speak other men's words, to follow other men's habits', the penalty for difference, he added, using the word Mill was to try to invest with the glow of creativity, was to be called 'eccentric'[79] The spectacle of modern manners, typically seen in the eighteenth century either in terms of a polite sociability or of corruption, evoked a post-Romantic ennui: 'that tyranny of the commonplace which seems to accompany civilization.'[80]

Such complaints became almost standard among intellectual liberals in the mid-century To celebrate the power of public opinion as above all beneficial, the great sanction against abuses, with the Press as its watch-dog, was, if not perhaps less common, certainly a less sophisticated view than it had

[77] *Works*, iv 114.
[78] James Mill, *Essay on Government* (London, 1820); Jack Lively and John Rees, *Utilitarian Logic and Politics: James Mill's 'Essay on Government' and Macaulay's Critique and the Ensuing Debate* (Oxford University Press, 1978), 94.
[79] 'Sir Robert Peel' (1856), in *Works*, iii. 243.  [80] Ibid.

been earlier when abuses were grosser Fears of its volatility, unpredictability, and excess, too, were less plausible in the mid-century In the critical year 1848 the nation had remained calm; its reward, one feels inclined to say, was to be sneered at as sluggish by its aspiring intellectual leaders. The sentimentalities and emotionalism of popular piety, 'the bray of Exeter Hall',[81] were risible to sophisticates, but hardly alarming, as the Methodist 'fanatics' and their 'conspiracy against common sense and orthodox Christianity' had been to so equable a spirit as Sydney Smith.[82] The descendants of the seventeenth-century sects, which had sometimes haunted eighteenth-century polite imaginations with the spectre of enthusiasm, had dwindled into Matthew Arnold's tea-drinking Philistines. Of course, it is misleading to package anything so diffuse and varied as the connotations of 'public opinion' too neatly into periods; nevertheless, the intellectual liberal fastidiousness and sense of claustrophobia of the mid-century has its own distinctive voice, whose most famous and most influential utterance is J S. Mill's essay *On Liberty*

The modern *régime* of public opinion is in an unorganised form, what the Chinese educational and political systems are in an organised; and unless individuality shall be able successfully to assert itself against this yoke, Europe will tend to become another China.[83]

This, perhaps the best-known pessimistic thought of that highly anxious work, introduces its two central and opposed concepts: public opinion and a self-developing, energetic, varied individuality; the danger, and the remedy It is to the latter, and its possible connections with earlier ways of thinking, that we now have to turn.

---

[81] Bagehot, in his essay on Adam Smith, quoting Macaulay Bagehot, *Works*, iii. 110.
[82] 'Methodism' (*Edinburgh Review*, 1808) in *The Works of the Rev. Sydney Smith* (London, 1839; new edn., 1869), 97
[83] J. S. Mill, *On Liberty*, in *Works*, xviii. 274.

# 4

## Autonomy and Self-realization
*From Independence to Individuality*

IN 1836 J. S. Mill published in the newly founded *London and Westminster Review* what became one of the best-known of his earlier essays, under the title 'Civilization' It belongs to a genre which had become firmly established in the eighteenth century· the assessment of the profit and loss entailed in the advance of civilization. To this genre belong some of the classic works of the earlier period: Rousseau's discourse on the progress of the arts and sciences, for example, and Adam Ferguson's *History of Civil Society*; it also provided, as we have seen earlier, the terms of much general political debate in eighteenth-century England and Scotland. To say this is not, of course, to make a point about the immediate intellectual antecedents of Mill's essay This is not the moment to attempt to rewrite his intellectual biography, even if I were capable of it. There are phrases in the essay which recall Rousseau,[1] just as there are others which, in their references to the moral enfeeblement of the modern world, and the incapacity of the middle classes for heroism and struggle, can sound prospectively like Nietzsche or Sorel;·but these, though they may point to unexpected affinities, are obviously not the stuff of detailed intellectual genealogy The authors explicitly acknowledged in Mill's essay are Tocqueville, Carlyle, and F D Maurice, though Coleridge, Goethe, and the Saint-Simonians are also tacitly present; the essay reflects the influence of Mill's organicist or corporatist phase.

Though Mill's essay is explicitly affirmative and optimistic —the disadvantages of civilization are corrigible—a casual reader would have been quite justified in regarding its author as a severe,

---

[1] e.g. 'a man's labour and capital are expended less in doing anything, than in persuading other people he has done it', 'Civilization', reprinted in *Mill's Essays on Literature and Society*, ed. J. B. Schneewind (London, 1965), 165–6.

even irritable, critic of its tendencies, rather than their celebrator. The central characteristics of civilization are co-operation and the division of labour, and while neither is condemned—indeed a further extension of co-operation is required—their effect is the submergence of the individual in the mass. In marked contrast both to a late eighteenth-century progressive Whig like John Millar, and to later visions of human progress put forward by liberal thinkers like Maine, Spencer, and Bagehot, Mill here, to some extent reflecting or refracting Tocqueville, sees the movement of human society as one from vigorous individualism to the torpor and uniformity of a state in which the individual is lost in the mass. The effect is often one of lamentation—an age of iron seems to be succeeded by one of brass. Modern man, or at least men in the comfortable classes, are morally weak; physically timid; humane but incapable of heroic exertion.[2] No longer do we see great virtues or great vices.[3]

Much of this, of course, is familiar from the later essay, *On Liberty*, though there is a significant difference to which we shall have to return. Putting questions of specific intellectual influence aside, there are several contexts in which Mill's lament or cultivated anxiety can be put apart from the perennial human disposition to look back to a past heroic age. There are—to take two related themes—Mill's enduring tendency to project his own early crisis, his loss of energy and will, on to society at large as a comprehensive historical paralysis, and, reinforcing it, the pervasive nineteenth-century Romantic disposition to lament the fading of life's primary colours, of passion and energy, and violent sensations, and to cultivate the ennui of a world grown grey and old. Mill's 'crisis' was as individual as his upbringing had been peculiar, but through it he knew the listlessness of the *enfant du siècle*. He read his Tocqueville on modern manners, one feels inclined to say, not exactly with aristocratic hauteur[4] but at least with something like a Byronic disdain. Wordsworth, not Byron, was his poet, and it would be hard, even if we had not his disclaimer, to picture Mill's

---

[2] *Mill's Essays*, ed. Schneewind, pp. 162–3.   [3] Ibid. 164.
[4] William Thomas has pointed out Mill's acknowledged gratitude that, through Bentham's tenancy of Ford Abbey and the Mill family's periods there, he had spent part of his youth in a medieval setting 'so unlike the mean and cramped externals of English middle class life' William Thomas, *Mill* (Oxford University Press, 1985), 2.

imagination ever dressed *en corsaire*: 'I was not in a frame of mind to derive any comfort from the vehement sensual passion of his Giaours'[5]—which must be the largest understatement of the *Autobiography* But it is worth recalling also the reason he gives for his preference: Byron's state of mind, in the exhaustion of its melancholy, 'was too like my own'.[6] There are certainly moments when, allowing for their ineradicable schoolmasterliness of tone, Mill's denunciation of provincial narrowness or of the grey wastes of contemporary middle-class manners are not far from those of a French Romantic of the 1830s and 1840s, flaunting his contempt for the bourgeoisie as a banner, and shuddering at the prospect of an American flattening of the social landscape—and Mill was intellectually in some ways more French than English. The apparent praise of eccentricity in *On Liberty* must have meant something, even if one cannot quite imagine Mill, like Gérard de Nerval, taking a lobster for a walk on a ribbon.

But this kind of context, of course, is not our concern here, nor is Mill's own intellectual biography I have mentioned it only lest what I shall go on to say should seem too peremptorily antiquarian, too much disposed to imply that there is nothing new under the sun, and too little to allow each generation its own idiom and concerns. For, of course, what is of interest to us here is, as I began by suggesting, the extent to which Mill's 'Civilization', consciously or not, attaches itself to an established eighteenth-century genre and echoes some of the latter's most familiar preoccupations. Mill's version of the social effects of the division of labour is sharply at variance with the most optimistic versions of the consequences of commercial society, to be found in the Scottish Enlightenment, as an enhanced independence: the individual was dependent on the impersonal force of the market rather than on the feudal magnate.[7] For Mill, at this point, the story runs otherwise. The self-sufficiency of the individual obliged to do much for himself is replaced by dependence on the specialized work of others. 'As civilization advances, every person becomes

---

[5] J. S. Mill, *Autobiography*, ed. J. Stillinger (Oxford University Press, 1971), 88.
[6] Ibid.
[7] This point is more fully developed below, pp. 90-1.

dependent, for more and more of what most nearly concerns him, not upon his own exertions, but upon the general arrangements of society ' The result is enfeeblement, and the chief remaining inducement 'to call forth energy of character' is the desire of wealth. Hence the effect of civilization is 'a relaxation of individual energy· or rather, the concentration of it within the narrower sphere of the individual's money-getting pursuits' [8]

There is much here which cannot avoid sounding like an eighteenth-century moralist, a critic of commercial society like Ferguson, or a Country Party theorist or republican Whig denouncing the corruption of public exertion by the indulgence of private interests (there may well be indirect lines of connection between Mill and 'Country' arguments, through Coleridge and Carlyle, but we cannot try to trace these in detail here). There is some change in characteristic diction, of course. Mill's immediate concern here is not directly political, and he speaks of 'individual energy' or 'character', rather than of virtue, patriotism, or public spirit. Yet to make too much of this distinction would be to underplay the extent to which the neo-classical republican ideal incorporated an ethic of self-fulfilment as well as a prescription for civic and constitutional liberty· political activity, in contrast to the specialized, servile works of trade, calls out the highest faculties of the free man. Much of Mill's vocabulary, particularly of condemnation, seems highly familiar from the earlier context, from the established rhetoric for speaking of civilization and its characteristic corruptions. The refinement and 'mildness of manners' associated with an advanced state of society have their long-established shadows: 'moral effeminacy', 'torpidity and cowardice', and a character 'relaxed and enervated' [9] It is true that the most immediate source of the evils, 'that the individual is lost and becomes impotent in the crowd',[10] strikes a different, distinctively nineteenth-century note. Yet when Mill speaks of the shielding of modern man from pain and danger by the division of labour, or of the unwillingness of noblemen to sacrifice 'their amusements and their ease' to the demands

---

[8] 'Civilization', in *Mill's Essays*, ed. Schneewind, p. 161.
[9] Ibid. 161-4.      [10] Ibid. 169

of public office,[11] the republican and Country echoes are loud and insistent: the citizen soldier and the republican statesman seduced from their responsibilities in the luxury of selfish leisure or the pursuit of private gain. We may hear too, if more faintly, the Country suspicion of a society based on credit and 'opinion' in Mill's belief that in the mass, which is the characteristic modern condition, men can no longer estimate each other rightly, and solid, known worth is replaced by puffing and quackery—a Carlylean theme this, of course.[12]

It cannot be said that Mill's proposed remedies—greater and more perfect combination among individuals' and 'national institutions of education'[13]—seem particularly well matched to the ills he has identified, even if they are no worse than Adam Smith's equivalent resort to education and the militia.[14] To seek in combination some alleviation of the individual's loss of power in the mass may be plausible, but that it, or even an improved system of national education, could do much to restore a lost self-sufficiency and capacity for heroic struggle seems less plausible. There seems, that is, an asymmetry between the Saint-Simonian and Coleridgian optimism and the Carlylean and, one is tempted to say, 'Country' pessimism. It is here that the equivalent argument in chapter three of *On Liberty* derived from Wilhelm von Humboldt's conception of individuality seems both more consonant with Mill's innate Protestantism and liberal individualism, and more aptly addressed to his central problem, even if less immediately practical.

The ideal presented in *On Liberty*, as we know, is that of a rich individuality, nurtured by free exposure to 'variety of experience' and diverse modes of life, issuing in an independence of mind and spirit which Mill presents both as the goal of individual human self-development and the guarantee of future social progress; it is the antidote to the mediocrity of a society made stagnant and narrowly oppressive by the pervasive pressure of average public opinion. Despite Mill's claim that the criterion he adopts in the essay is 'utility in

[11] Ibid. 162-3.   [12] Ibid. 165-9.   [13] Ibid. 169
[14] Donald Winch, *Adam Smith's Politics: An Essay in Historiographic Revision* (Cambridge University Press, 1978), 113.

the largest sense',[15] the central place he gives to 'individuality' clearly marks a significant development from a liberalism grounded in strict utilitarian theory; it came, in retrospect, to seem a turning-point. As L. T Hobhouse wrote in his manifesto of Liberalism half a century later, Mill 'spans the old and the new liberalism';[16] it was the transition from a hedonistic ethic of want satisfaction to one of the fullest possible realization of the whole self.[17]

Mill introduced the concept of a cultivated individuality, as was customary with him, both as a conceptual novelty and a foreign import, borrowed directly, through substantial quotation, from the recent (1854) translation of Humboldt's early essay on the powers of the state.[18] It was the late eighteenth-century German, Hellenistic concept of *Bildung*, autonomous self-cultivation and self-development. In one sense the (relative) novelty, in England, was genuine, though Mill himself had been attracted to the notion of many-sided self-development, epitomized above all for the nineteenth century by Goethe, since the time of his mental crisis thirty years earlier. The word 'individuality', adopted as a key term by Humboldt's translator Joseph Coulthard, had, incidentally, been used by Burke, at different times with a positive and a pejorative sense, the latter corresponding roughly to the later 'individualism' [19] 'Self-culture', or 'cultivation',[20] can be seen as the opposite of what the eighteenth century called 'rudeness' But the eighteenth century's most common antitheses for rudeness or barbarism, 'refinement' and 'politeness', carry connotations not of the

---

[15] *On Liberty*, in *Collected Works of John Stuart Mill*, ed. J. M. Robson (Toronto, 1977), xviii. 224.

[16] L. T Hobhouse, *Liberalism* (London, 1911), 58.

[17] The other major influence here, of course, was the Idealism of T H. Green.

[18] Wilhelm von Humboldt, *The Sphere and Duties of Government*, trans. Joseph Coulthard (London, 1854). Humboldt's essay was written in the early 1790s but not published in full until 1852.

[19] 'Individuality is left out of their scheme of government. The state is all in all.' 'Regicide Peace', in *The Writings and Speeches of Edmund Burke*, 12 vols. (London, 1900), v. 375. For the pejorative use see below, ch. 6 n. 25. The fact that Burke could apply the same word both to what the Revolution destroyed and to what it represented hints at the paradox we shall have to consider in the next chapter, that individualism could offer a threat to individuality

[20] e.g. the ironic defence by the protagonist of Clough's *Amours de Voyage* of his reluctance to risk his life in the cause of Roman republicanism: 'Still, individual culture is also something.' A. H. Clough, *Amours de Voyage* (London, 1849).

nourishment of individuality (though this was not quite Matthew Arnold's concept either) but of the smoothing of rough edges and the purging of grossness by a restraining sociability.[21] 'Genius', in its eighteenth-century sense of something peculiar and distinctive to oneself, carried some of the connotations of 'individuality', but it referred rather to a bent of talent than to the whole self. 'Singularity', like eccentricity, conveyed a suggestion of raised eyebrows.

So far, we seem confronted in Mill's 'individuality' and 'self-development' by a concept both modern and exotic. But even cultural imports are seldom as novel as they appear, or as Mill clearly liked them to be. They have to be assimilated, if they are to 'take', to the established language of moral and political appraisal, with its overlapping, subtly related senses of approval and rejection, and to gradual shifts of usage and nuance, with the same words differently employed, or others gradually coming to perform similar but not identical functions. Sheldon Rothblatt has written illuminatingly and relevantly, concerning this, of the cultural transition and the changing social context reflected in the high valuation attached, in the nineteenth century, to 'character', compared with the eighteenth century's exaltation of 'society',[22] while Stefan Collini has recently explored the political significance of 'character' and its affiliates, particularly 'manliness', as a pervasive value in Victorian liberal discourse, including, of course, Mill's *On Liberty*, and pointed to some of the differences from its eighteenth-century precursors.[23]

*On Liberty* was in part overtly a protest against the smug narrowness of the mid-Victorian idea of character—its 'Hebraism' and 'Philistinism', in the phrases coined by Arnold, expounding his own version of Hellenism. But we have for

---

[21] On this see Sheldon Rothblatt, *Tradition and Change in English Liberal Education* (London, 1976), esp. chs. 2, 7
[22] Ibid. 102-3, 115-16, 133-4.
[23] Stefan Collini, 'The Idea of "Character" in Victorian Political Thought', *Transactions of the Royal Historical Society*, 5th ser. 35 (1985), 29-50. Collini's stimulating article deals, often in more detail, with many of the points raised in this lecture, and I shall not be able to reproduce, in the present context, many of the subtleties in the distinctions he makes. In acknowledging my debts to it I have also to thank him for allowing me to read his unpublished paper ' "Manly Fellows" Fawcett, Stephen and the Liberal Temper', given to the conference on Fawcett at Trinity Hall, Cambridge, in December 1984.

the most part to use the established language of our contemporaries and borrow its resonances, and Mill could hardly avoid testifying to the power of their idea of character, over them and over himself.[24] He was not, after all, whatever he may have said, telling his countrymen something wholly unknown or even altogether uncongenial; he was merely trying rather half-heartedly to add a German and Hellenistic gracenote to something they already knew and believed in: self-direction, human autonomy, and self-reliance. He was also, in his own way, endorsing, at the level of the clash and mutual influence of personalities, a familiar and cherished concept: the market, where one competed and exchanged, and all but the slack and the unenterprising benefited. Neither he nor Humboldt, in advocating variety of experience as necessary to the development of character, was giving a licence to self-indulgence, though suspicious contemporaries may sometimes have thought so, but rather providing another element to the familiar, strenuous notion of competition: in this case the bracing encounter of contending styles of life and personality [25]

Humboldt had emphasised not only diversity of experience but also the essential autonomy of each individual in making his own synthesis. The roots of his thought here were Rousseauist and Kantian—man must above all be self-directed. It was a moral and political concept easily rendered into the slang of nineteenth-century English liberalism,[26] and at times this is what Mill in *On Liberty* seems to be doing—using a foreign idea, as usual, to browbeat his countrymen for their narrowness, while simultaneously domesticating this exotic pagan, German, and aesthetic import into titles by Samuel Smiles: 'Character' and 'Self-Help' His readers, as Mill recognized, were hardly likely to object to the desirability of

---

[24] Collini, 'The Idea of "Character" ', p. 31.

[25] I have tried to set out the political implications Humboldt drew from the concept of *Bildung*, in Wilhelm von Humboldt, *The Limits of State Action*, ed. and trans. J. W Burrow (Cambridge University Press, 1969), Introduction. This is the same work as the one used by Mill, translated under another title closer to the original, *The Sphere and Duties of Government*, trans. Joseph Coulthard (London, 1854).

[26] Collini speaks aptly here of 'the unreflective Kantianism of Victorian moral commonplaces' ('The Idea of "Character" ', p. 34), though he also makes the point that the nature of the contemporary criticisms of Mill's essay indicates the distance between *Bildung* and 'character', ibid. 38.

'originality' or even, he might have added, of 'an energetic character',[27] though praise of 'eccentricity' was admittedly a bold strike. But it is the contrasts which strike us as most familiar, and not merely in the context of mid-Victorian England: 'mediocrity', 'uniformity', 'torpid', 'indolent'[28] — they are, for example, the characteristics of Gibbon's corrupted Romans, and the diction is the same. Again we have been led back, via a Continental detour, to the moral vocabulary of the eighteenth-century civic humanist.[29]

Nor is this altogether surprising, because the Country Party language of public virtue and Mill's embattled progressive liberalism have a good deal in common; a strenuous moralism and an acute sociological anxiety The first, however, we can now begin to note, is focused on corruption, the latter on stagnation.[30] In this both are very unlike the pragmatic language of adjustment to the changing character of civil society, which allowed for a range of temperamental variation from the easygoing to the impatient, characteristic of the Scottish-inspired progressive Whiggism of the earlier years of the nineteenth century Of course, we are speaking of pure types; in practice, as we saw in the case of Jeffrey's civic moralizing, there was an interplay between 'Country' and 'progressive' attitudes as there had been in the eighteenth century But for the moment, in speaking of similarities of conception, tone, and function, in languages — Country Party and mid-Victorian liberal — between which there seems no immediate historical connection, we can speak purely taxonomically Both, we may say, differ from progressive Whiggism in making their concern lest the moral fibre on which all depends should slacken not occasional but perennial and constitutive, in their respective political diagnoses and exhortations. In both cases, because we are invited to think of a social agency on which the whole fate of the polity or

---

[27] *On Liberty*, in *Collected Works*, xviii. 264, 267
[28] Ibid. 262, 263, 266, 268.
[29] On Gibbon's relation to the civic-humanist tradition, see J. G. A. Pocock, 'Between Machiavelli and Hume: Gibbon as Civic Humanist and Philosophical Historian', in G. W Bowersock, John Clive, and Stephen R. Graubard (eds.), *Edward Gibbon and the Fall of the Roman Empire* (London, 1977)
[30] On both these points, see Collini, 'The Idea of "Character"', p. 42.

society turns there is an accompanying anxiety Public virtue and individuality are conditions of social health which may easily be lost. To sustain them calls for a constant exertion of moral energy; to allow this to weaken is a fatal enervation. The consequence is the loss of the most cherished social good, which for the eighteenth-century constitutionalist is 'public liberty' and for Mill 'social progress' The distinction between the two is important, and we will have to consider it again later. But in each case the feared final state, the collapse or enervation of energy and will, is referred to in similar terms. In the eighteenth century the opposite of public liberty is often an Asiatic, or, more especially, 'Turkish' servitude.[31] For Mill the antithesis of the state of progressive social energy, fuelled by freedom of thought and speech, and the vigorous cultivation of a spontaneous individuality, is 'Chinese stationariness' [32]

To understand the affiliations of these concepts better we need to attend more fully, first of all, to the resonances of 'virtue' in its eighteenth-century sense. The common verbal root of 'virtue' and 'virility' in the Latin *vir* is one which, in our usage, has dwindled into an etymological curiosity In the Machiavellian notion of *virtus*, *virtù*, the mainstay of the free republic, from which the English republican Whig and Country Party conception of political virtue derived, the idea of virility was central. Commentators have drawn attention to the initial intrinsic connection of *virtù* with the notion of imposing one's will on Fortune, Fortuna, who, fickle and wayward, is invariably portrayed as a woman. *Virtù* gives mastery over the flux of circumstance and one's own weakness, by self-control, daring, self-assertion. The end is the classical one of glory or fame, and when *virtù* is required of the ordinary citizen of the republic, the glory or greatness is no longer simply that of the individual but of the state. *Virtù* becomes public spirit, patriotism, the sacrifice of private interest to civic duty, which includes political participation, but also still, significantly, courage, martial virtue, and energy It was in this sense that

---

[31] The classic 18th-cent. source for notions of 'Asiatic despotism' became Montesquieu. See Montesquieu, *The Spirit of the Laws*, trans. Thomas Nugent (New York, 1949), bk. III, 8–11, bk. IV, 3; bk. V, 14–19

[32] *On Liberty*, in *Collected Works*, xviii. 273–4. This contrast is developed more fully in the next lecture.

the Romans owed their empire, initially, to their virtue.[33] A citizen army is the guarantee both against conquest from abroad and despotism at home. Freedom is not private self-indulgence, which figures as a form of corruption, but full participation, as a free citizen, in the public life of a free state. The sexual connotations of virtue in this sense are by no means lost in the eighteenth century 'Effeminacy' is frequently cited as the antithesis of public spirit and energy, in the standard attacks on 'luxury' It figures constantly in Gibbon's *Decline and Fall* as an explanation of the decline of states, above all, of course, of Rome. Luxury is 'effeminate' Of course, it will not do to exaggerate the importance of the directly sexual connotation; Gibbon did not, like the Victorian schoolmaster of legend, refer the decline of Rome to sexual indulgence. But the blending of political meaning and sexual resonance is worth stressing if it recalls the Renaissance and Classical origins of the idea, and the martial as well as civic qualities of the *vir* A despot, in eighteenth-century idiom, ruled over a nation of 'slaves', and slaves, in the political sense, are effeminate, lacking the virile spirit and energy to fight for their liberties. 'Asiatic despotism' and 'Asiatic effeminacy' were closely associated eighteenth-century clichés.

For the Victorians, virtue, taken into Anglo-Saxon as manliness,[34] was a concept by no means without political or even egalitarian connotations, epitomized in the proletarian affectations of Kingsley's 'baccy' or Stephen coaching his college eight in the towpath language of the bargee, or, in fiction, by the brusquerie of Thackeray's *déclassé* country gentleman, George Warrington, in *Pendennis*. Such mannerisms were an advertisement of independence and rugged seriousness, showing contempt for dandyism, for the fashionable glossiness and smartness which Carlyle—an important influence—had christened 'gigmanship', and for

---

[33] This account closely follows Quentin Skinner, *Machiavelli* (Oxford University Press, 1981), 28–9, 53–4.

[34] 'Manhood' had not quite the same doctrinaire implications. For the Victorian concept of manliness generally, see particularly David Newsome, *Godliness and Good Learning* (London, 1961), section IV, and Norman Vance, *The Sinews of the Spirit: The Ideal of Christian Manliness in Victorian Literature and Religious Thought* (Cambridge University Press, 1985). Also Collini, 'The Idea of "Character"', pp. 45–9

what the Georgians had called servility, and the nineteenth century, more often, 'toadying' or 'flunkeyism' [35] But 'manly' (or sometimes 'masculine') had long had a significance that was political as well as personal, as when Gibbon spoke of the Goths' 'manly spirit of freedom', or when we find Acton, a century later, referring to 'masculine notions of limited authority and conditional obedience' [36] 'Manly', for Georgians and Victorians alike, had connotations of self-mastery and sexual restraint, firmness, candour, and independence. And independence was the fundamental condition of political health in the 'Country' rhetoric of the eighteenth century, as for Mill it was the key to social energy· independence, in the one case, of ministerial influence, in the other, of a public opinion now seen as the ultimate source of power.

It was, as Professor Pocock has shown us, James Harrington who, writing in England in the Machiavellian civic-humanist tradition, connected the crucial notion of the armed citizen as the champion of liberty with that of the independent freeholder, the self-sufficient owner of landed property [37] The contrast was with feudalism; the armed vassal fought at the behest of another, the freeholder by his own will. In doing so Harrington forged the connection of Machiavellian civic *virtù* with the English eighteenth-century concept of 'independence' In the civic, neo-Machiavellian tradition, it is not political liberty that exists to protect property, it is property that has to provide the basis for the exercise of political liberty, which is the highest function of the free man. Harrington, in connecting civic virtue with the independence conferred by freehold property, made the Machiavellian notion available in the context of a representative, parliamentary political system, identifying the freeholders with the House of Commons and particularly, of course, with the County Members. Pocock, in *The Machiavellian Moment*, has traced now that it provided, for

[35] The source for the former (also, sometimes, 'toadyism'), 'toad-eating', was an 18th-cent. term. It was, above all, Carlyle who allegorized such qualities as '-isms'
[36] Edward Gibbon, *The History of the Decline and Fall of the Roman Empire*, ed. J. B. Bury, 7 vols. (6th edn., London, 1912), 1. 58. Cf. 'The manly pride of the Romans', which had scorned the ostentation of the East, ibid. ii., 159; Acton, *The History of Freedom and other Essays*, ed. J. N. Figgis (London, 1909), 45.
[37] J. G. A. Pocock (ed.), *The Political Works of James Harrington* (Cambridge University Press, 1977), Editor's introduction.

more than half a century, the grounds of opposition to a political system that worked essentially through patronage, clientage, and dependence. After the passing of the Septennial Act, the members of Parliament seemed, not without cause, increasingly in danger of becoming not representatives but a separate class of professional politicians, lured and bribed by places and emoluments, and becoming, through them, pliant tools of the exective. To preserve liberty and the balance of the constitution by strengthening the independence of the members of Parliament, by shorter parliaments, the exclusion of placemen, and in some cases by proposals for increasing the proportion of County Members compared with the political clients who sat for pocket boroughs became the staple of opposition political rhetoric; so also, again with Machiavellian and Harringtonian warrant, did attacks on a standing army, for which the Country gentry had largely to pay, through the land tax, and the exaltation instead of the idea of a national militia as a training in citizenship and as the guardian of constitutional freedom. It is plausible to see nineteenth-century notions of 'character' as the adaptation of the eighteenth-century political conception of 'independence' to a wider, less exclusive, more mobile, more competitive, and certainly no longer necessarily landed society The newer term is less directly political; in the long run political liberty may depend on it, but its field of exercise is primarily 'society' rather than politics. But the chief difference from 'independence' or the political sense of 'virtue' is a different relation to competition and to history Both are strenuous, but one is thought of as preservative, the other as dynamic. The Harringtonian freeholder enjoyed his independence partly because he did not have to compete in the market place to make his way· his field of competition was military The nineteenth-century man of character was most typically thought of as forging that character *through* struggle, through competition.[38] And whereas the price of failure in the former case was the loss of constitutional liberty, in the latter it is seen by Mill as stagnation, submission to the inertia of mediocrity

---

[38] Collini, 'The Idea of "Character" ', pp. 39-40, 42-3. Cf. Rothblatt, *Tradition and Change*, ch. 10, on the growth of competition in education.

But there is a further and less obvious analogy between the Harringtonian freeholder and the concept of individuality deployed in *On Liberty*; it lies in the fact that the Country ideal embodies a kind of resistance to specialization and the division of labour. The independent freeholder, the County representative, though he *is* a representative and not simply a citizen exercising his vote as a free member of the *polis* in the *agora*, has, nevertheless, in the neo-classical, neo-Harringtonian conception, an important integrity It is the integrity of self-sufficiency; he is free both as a landholder and as a political agent, in contrast to the merchant dependent on the whims of the market, or the fundholder or the placeman, who is a parasite on government. By contrast, what is denounced can be seen as forms of specialization, of the division of labour. In the standing army the citizen and soldier are separated: the latter is now a hireling, serving for wages. In the political placeman, the citizen and politician are separated; the latter is now a professional, a distinct class of man, finding his interest not with that of the generality of freeholders of his locality whom the County member represents, but with the executive, the career-politicians.

But the eighteenth century also witnessed, of course, in the thought of the Scottish Enlightenment, the emergence of a kind of defence of specialization as an intrinsic characteristic of a modern civilized society. It is sometimes only a partial defence—the civic tradition still exerted its pull—but it is vital because it characteristically shifts the notion of independence away from the integrity of the landed freeholder to the market, to commerce rather than land. Independence is now the absence of the personal dependence which characterizes for all but a few the relations of rural society; independence is dependence only on the impersonal laws of the market. In the *Wealth of Nations* Smith contrasts the feudal landlord on whom many are directly dependent, as retainers, with the same magnate in a money economy Indirectly, by spending money in the market, he helps to maintain many more men than before, as artisans and middlemen. 'He generally contributes, however, but a very small proportion to that of each, . Though he contributes, therefore to the maintenance of them all, they are all more or less independent of him, because generally they can all be maintained without him.'[39]

But it is only one aspect of commerce to promote independence. Its other aspect is in some degree to depreciate the value attached to the kind of independence enjoyed by the freeholding participant in a free polity As we saw earlier, it makes society, rather than polity, the locus of value and the school of self-education, in a less rugged, more polished complex of values than Machiavellian virtue.[40] The degree of *mutual* dependence, trust, and polite intercourse, necessarily brought with commerce, could be seen as itself education, polishing the rough edges of the independent personality, eradicating prejudices and promoting liberal and enlightened views. In the eighteenth century, 'economy' is not set against 'society', but at the moral level is often virtually fused with it. Pocock points out, as an example of this, the use of 'commerce', 'intercourse', and 'conversation', as terms for both social and sexual exchange.[41] In speaking of nations, 'commerce' and 'intercourse' are also interchangeable, and both imply friendly and pacific relations, in contrast to the warlike presuppositions of Machiavellian republicanism. It was possible too to speak of 'the commerce of the sexes' with no implication of a sneer. The social virtues of politeness, tolerance, the willingness to be improved in the company of others have partially replaced, as it were, the political virtues of public spirit, patriotism, and martial valour The independence cherished by the republican and Country Party tradition could now come to seem narrow, even uncouth. To Macaulay, as a metropolitan Whig, strongly touched by the influences of the Scottish Enlightenment, the County Member of Parliament is always a relative of Squire Western: an unlettered, narrow-minded boor One of the points in common between James Mill

---

[39] Adam Smith, *Wealth of Nations* (Oxford University Press, 1976), 420.
[40] Above, ch. 2.
[41] 'Cambridge Paradigms', in Istvan Hont and Michael Ignatieff (eds.), *Wealth and Virtue: The Shaping of Political Economy in the Scottish Enlightenment* (Cambridge University Press, 1983), 241. On the general themes touched on above, see the essays, particularly, by Phillipson and by Ignatieff, ibid.

and Macaulay was their exaltation of the urban middle classes.[42]

But the transformation of values was only partial, and sometimes a matter for unease and ambivalence. Fears of 'effeminacy', corruption, loss of public spirit are still vigorous among such representatives of the Scottish Enlightenment as Ferguson and Millar, and even Smith. Nor is the issue of specialization and the division of labour always straightforward; Smith's remarks in the *Wealth of Nations* on the narrowing effects of the division of labour in manufacture have become famous, while in the *Lectures on Jurisprudence* we are told that 'the minds of men are contracted and rendered incapable of elevation. Education is despised, or at least neglected, and heroic spirit is almost utterly extinguished.'[43]

Optimism about the prospects of commercial society or civilization, in fact, required the maintenance of a kind of balance between energy and refinement, between independence and sociability It was not one the leading figures of the Scottish Enlightenment always found easy to maintain, and by the time we reach Mill, the balance seems decisively to tilt in a way that inevitably takes him back to the hortatory tone and even the historical pessimism of the republican language of civic virtue. That language was, of course, a neo-classical one, and it would perhaps be easy to make a historical leap too quickly here, when, for example, we find Mill quoting Sterling to the effect that 'Pagan self-assertion' is one of the elements of human worth, as well as 'Christian self-denial'[44] 'Pagan self-assertion' is, after all, a very fair description of Machiavellian *virtù*. It is not Machiavellian here, of course, but it is neo-classical. In the sources of Mill's essay it is not the Roman stoic version of the classical heritage, which, with some reference to Sparta, fed Renaissance civic humanism, Augustan Country Party opposition, and the French Jacobins, which is uppermost. It is, as we saw, a Hellenistic paganism, in origin aesthetic rather

---

[42] On the extent of their common ground, see Winch, 'The Cause of Good Government', in Stefan Collini, Donald Winch, and John Burrow, *That Noble Science of Politics: A Study in Nineteenth-century Intellectual History* (Cambridge University Press, 1983), 122.
[43] Quoted in Winch, *Adam Smith's Politics*, p. 82. Cf. ibid. 83, 116–18.
[44] *On Liberty*, in *Collected Works*, xviii. 265.

than political, and its proximate source is late eighteenth-century Germany The inspiration is not Roman but Greek.
Its relevance to what we have been considering so far is that, as an ideal for humanity, it is among other things a protest against specialization and the division of labour, the supposed fragmentation of modern man, and a call for the restoration of a lost integrity;[45] not, understandably in the Germany of the princes, through political participation, but through private aesthetic self-cultivation. In this yearning for self-fulfilment through the restoration of an integrity and autonomy supposedly achieved in the classical *polis*, there is at least some common ground between Machiavellian civic humanism and German aesthetic paganism, so that Rousseau, for example, could play a role in the transmission of the first and in the formation of the second. The myth of Sparta or republican Rome and the myth of Athens were rival models, but compared with modern Europe they naturally presented similarities. The possibility of fusing patriotic civic participation and a cultivated roundedness of personality, for all the obvious contrast between the political and martial virtues stressed in the first, and the aesthetic individualism, in its German neo-Hellenic form, of the second, could be a tantalizing one. Humboldt, in his later public career, could be thought of as having achieved it.

Humboldt, like the young Mill, had been reacting against the aridity of an excessive rationalism. Politically, the two essays addressed widely different circumstances. Writing in a context of Enlightenment absolutism, Humboldt had been concerned above all to limit the powers of the state; Mill was preoccupied, under the influence of Tocqueville, with the tyranny of public opinion. But Mill's own early domestic life had given him a taste of benevolent despotism; overdriven and, as he felt, desiccated, he had responded to Romantic notions of organic growth and variety, just as Humboldt had tried to assimilate the raw individual self-assertion and emotionalism of the *Sturm und Drang* to an Enlightenment concern for order, by subsuming both under a metaphor of harmonious self-development drawn from a Hellenizing aesthetics. Apollo and

---

[45] e.g. F Schiller, *Letters on the Aesthetic Education of Mankind*, trans. R. Snell (London, 1954), 37–9

Dionysius as complementary deities were launched on their influential careers in German thought at the end of the eighteenth century.[46]

But Mill in *On Liberty* understandably exploits only a part—the more public aspect—of the possibilities of German neo-classicism, turning Humboldt's concept into something distinctly English, liberal, and mid-Victorian. Privately he acknowledged, not surprisingly, that he found the aesthetics of personal development, the ideal of harmony supposedly exemplified in Goethe, not what was required: 'Not symmetry, but bold, free expansion in all directions is demanded by the needs of modern life and the instincts of the modern mind.'[47] It is vigour and cultural *laissez-faire* that are stressed in Mill's essay. His own fear at this point was not primarily specialization but entropy—the latter, admittedly, also an anxiety of Humboldt's. Mill even turned the emphasis on variety into something rather more cerebral, and it is hard to consider the endorsement of strong emotion and wide experience, and even Mill's anxious sense that without these stimulants he, and therefore society at large, might fall into the apathetic state he had once endured, as other than theoretical.

But the call of social responsibility was always peremptory. He professed to admire the Goethian ideal of 'many-sidedness'—his use of the phrase is a translation of *Vielseitigkeit*. But for him, one feels, it was most familiarly exemplified in terms of *opinion* rather than personality.[48] Endorsing the social value of diversity of opinion, as he does in *On Liberty*, was something which native protestant as well as scientific predilections could readily assimilate. It struck home to him particularly because his flirtation with Comtism had once brought him close to a corporate, 'scientific' authoritarianism. Variety of experience was a more exotic notion; Mill had experienced the aridity of a life devoted solely to public causes, but he was no heir of the *Sturm und Drang*

---

[46] Humboldt, *Limits of State Action*, Editor's introduction, pp. xi-xvii, xxix-xxx, xxxvii-xxxviii.
[47] Diary entry, 6 Feb. 1854, in Schneewind (ed.), *Mill's Essays*, p. 351.
[48] This point is made by Shirley Letwin in *The Pursuit of Certainty* (Cambridge University Press, 1965), 237-8.

There is, in fact, a certain innocence about Mill's principled acceptance of diversity of experience; it was blithe, with an imperviousness to any sense of cultural peril; the bracing effects of competition would ensure general health, while the concept of 'other-regarding' actions safeguarded the claims of public morality But Humboldt's ideal staked poise and identity in the whirl of experience; to be prepared to prove all knowledge on the pulses was no light undertaking. In cultural eclecticism, and in the morality of the aesthete — the pursuit of the exquisite, exotic, or passionate sensation in the cause of self-development — there was a threat to moral rigour and will of which Mill seems scarcely aware. Others were less innocent and public-spirited, and the German Hellenic paganism of Winckelmann and Goethe lived on not only in aspects of *On Liberty* and Arnold's *Culture and Anarchy* but in Pater's *Renaissance* and *Marius the Epicurean*, and hence in the aestheticism of the *fin de siècle*.

The intellectual moods of the last decades of the century were given a peculiar intensity and unease both by the aesthete's claim to all experience as right and by the imperialist's daily exposure to the jarring encounters of alien cultures. There was an exhaustion of cultural surfeit, the wearied eyelids of Pater's world-historical *Gioconda*, as well as of Mill's early undernourishment. Such enervation, the sense of an almost intolerable weight of cultural accumulation, suggested Roman analogies to Pater,[49] just as the imperialist sometimes found both historical camaraderie and unease in contemplating the *pax Romana*. The decadent bravado of the aesthete, and what seemed the development of an offensively opulent plutocracy, gave a new pointedness to images of Roman luxury and historical decline, and the suggested remedies often have a familiar ring. The strenuousness of what we may call the 'radical right' towards the end of the century, the strident patriotism, the calls for conscription, the cult of stoicism, and public service seem at times to echo the themes of the Machiavellian civic tradition, including self-conscious parallels

---

[49] 'As in some vast intellectual museum, all its manifold products were intact and in their places', *Marius the Epicurean* (London, 1885), ch. xi.

with Rome. The military virtues were back in favour, for

> what is your boasting worth
> If ye grudge a year of service to the lordliest life on earth?[50]

Georgian enthusiasts for a militia could have applauded.

Such preoccupations reached their apogee, of course, at the end of the century, in the iconography of imperialism, in composite images from Kipling, Newbolt, Lady Butler, and the *Illustrated London News*, blending heroic self-reliance, patriotic dedication and self-sacrifice, and the self-imposed rigours of austerity· Scott in the Antarctic, Gordon in the desert; the lone subaltern with his native platoon, narrowing his eyes to the flicker of the heliograph, as the last link with the civilized world of mess-jackets, women, and polite conversation. It was a role which combined devotion to duty and testing isolation, and it is the latter which, compared with the eighteenth century, strikes the new note, reflecting not only the realities of imperialism but the Victorian idea of character involving something more than 'independence', incorporating post-Romantic and Protestant elements which made a measure of solitary testing intrinsic to it, and partially distinguished it from the Roman and Renaissance conception of the life of civic virtue.[51] The hero of imperialism was partly a new species, what Stefan Collini aptly calls '*homo Newboltiensis*', compounded of older elements, a young Spartan educated for civic virtue by 'the artificial provision of adversity' in compulsory games.[52] He had been developing since the 1860s. The deliberate provision of such tests, English education's gift to her upper-class sons, begins, as we know, in the second half of the nineteenth century, as an essential feature in the formation of the public school ethos. Its antithesis was that by now old-fashioned Whiggism whose ethic, shaped in the course of the eighteenth century, was civilized rather than civic, and which placed salons and the society of women among the chief agents of education;[53] Newbolt's subalterns had characteristically known little of

---

[50] 'The Islanders' in *Collected Verse of Rudyard Kipling* (London, 1912), 307
[51] Collini, 'The Idea of "Character"', p. 47      [52] Ibid. 48, 49
[53] Rothblatt, *Tradition and Change*, pp. 87–90.

either, and would strongly have suspected both as inimical to moral fibre.

Analogies between J. S. Mill and Sir Henry Newbolt have not, admittedly, been part of the regular currency of cultural history Yet briefly and as a way of unsettling our preconceptions, we might ponder a moment, forgetting that its author was Mill, the various possible implications of a work in which energy is exalted and mass opinion despised. I am not making a point about unexpected individual affinities here, much less, of course, about 'influence', but one about the ways in which motifs in a culture float, adhere, and recombine in diverse ways. Pater too, as I have suggested, offers Mill an unintended and no doubt unconscious cousinship. Nor are the two strands, rugged and exquisite, always sharply distinct. Loneliness and defiance could be the aesthete's lot as well as the imperialist's, and homosexuality could be Spartan or Athenian. To the Nietzschian aesthete the hardships and austerities of ostensibly patriotic self-sacrifice could appeal as another form of intense experience: there are elements of this in both of the great popular heroes of the First World War, Rupert Brooke and T E. Lawrence. We can hardly imagine Mill approving, but the lines of cultural inheritance he conscientiously, and in his own view defiantly, domesticated in *On Liberty* as mid-Victorian liberalism, were more highly charged and suggestive than he, perhaps fortunately, can ever have realized.

Let me conclude with a parable, a scene, in fact, from a novel, published in 1901 Inevitably its author is Kipling, in whom the strands we have considered are so oddly combined: imperialist, and stepson, as it were, through Burne-Jones and Cormell Price, of the Pre-Raphaelite rather than Hellenic version of late-Victorian aestheticism; celebrator of patriotic duty and of anarchic individualism, trumpeter of empire, and author of its 'Recessional'

Empire provided the testing ground of will not only in the obvious sense that it was sometimes dangerous, but in the sense that the world to which imperialism gave access was immensely culturally various and often seductive. Here the two elements of Mill's 'individuality', cultural experimentation and strength of character, could fall apart. In late nineteenth- and early

98    *Autonomy and Self-realization*

twentieth-century England, the ultimate failure of will, civic virtue, and character, was epitomized not, as for its Georgian predecessor, by the free citizen corrupted by luxury, but by the European, as the phrase went, 'gone native' For, in going native one betrayed simultaneously two usually contrasted eighteenth-century ideals, patriotic virtue and civilization. It was an eighteenth-century anxiety too, though collectively rather than individually focused: 'luxury' had strong oriental connotations. The 'nabob' was an image of corruption in eighteenth-century politics, while for Gibbon a notable symptom of the decline of Rome was the orientalization of its governing class. But in the later nineteenth century the imperialist seemed to become culturally vulnerable in a new way, with the waning of the Christian earnestness which had inspired so many of the heroes of imperialism in the mid-century, and with this attenuation the loss of the most obvious resources of cultural resistance. The residue of that earnestness could invest disturbing encounters with the culturally alien with the metaphysical terrors of the Marabar caves:[54] it was scarcely possible simply to reorder the nabob's cushions and curled slippers. What if the world were ultimately meaningless, a flux of experience given meaning only by will and action? Diversity and exoticism of experience raised the possibility of being overwhelmed, of a literal loss of identity, cultural and psychological.[55] Greed for experience was, after all, a Romantic notion which had always lain close to images of delirium, of the strayed reveller, and Faust on the Brocken. The most obvious defences were a philistine insensitivity and a stoic sense of duty which would once have been called public virtue.

Kipling's Kim, the boy who lives between two worlds and responds eagerly and imitatively to the cultural medley of Indian life, is at one point given a test.[56] The setting is an antique shop that provides the cover for the British secret

[54] E. M. Forster, *A Passage to India* (London, 1924).
[55] For a sensitive discussion of this see Eric Stokes, ' "The Voice of the Hooligan" Kipling and the Commonwealth Experience', in N. McKendrick (ed.), *Historical Perspectives: Studies in English Thought and Society in Honour of J. H. Plumb* (London, 1974).
[56] Rudyard Kipling, *Kim* (London, 1901), ch. ix.

agent in Simla. The antique shop, incidentally, provided other nineteenth-century writers besides Kipling with a disturbing image of cultural eclecticism suggesting delirium; Balzac's hero in *Le Peau de chagrin* is led to his Faustian bargain through one. Kim's senses are confused by the multiplicity of objects in the shop, a phantasmagoria of oriental cultures. An attempt is made to hypnotize him. It fails. He clings to reason and empiricism; his will prevails; the jug *was* broken. Kim, in Kipling's terms, that is, remains a European, though, by his upbringing and imitativeness, always alone at the intersection of cultures and suffering conflicts of loyalty The Hindu boy in the shop is better than Kim at memorizing objects but he is easily hypnotized. He is also, in the eighteenth-century phrase, effeminate: pretty and weak. 'Soft' is the word Kipling several times uses. Gibbon would have understood the parable; so too would Humboldt or Nietzsche. And Mill? —well, it was not quite India as he was used to thinking about it, but his father had strongly disapproved of overenthusiastic orientalists.[57]

Why have I chosen to end with a scene apparently so far from British politics and political theory? Some of the themes I have referred to could no doubt be illustrated from more predictable sources. In Bosanquet's *Philosophical Theory of the State* or Hobhouse's *Morals in Evolution* we find, for example, variously displayed, notions of a successful comprehensiveness of thought and experience, embodied for the former in a Hegelian Idea of the State. There are other analogies with Mill's fears of social entropy through mediocrity, sometimes coloured, in the later period, by Social Darwinism and notions of race.[58] But if the implication of my choice, for a concluding illustration, of a work of literature set in an exotic land is that the themes we have chiefly been considering— patriotic *virtù*, corruption, individuality, and character—have at last become marginal and exotic, largely losing their long connection with political liberty, that was its intention. In an age of mass politics, *virtù* had become apolitical, a form of

---

[57] James Mill, *The History of British India*, 3 vols. (London, 1817), vol. 1, bk. 2.
[58] Particularly C. H. Pearson, *National Life and Character: A Forecast* (London, 1893).

specialization like any other, and one which, in so far as it is any general use to the state, is employed not in sustaining the liberty of the republic, but in guarding the frontiers of the empire it has won.

# 5
## Balance and Diversity
### *From Roman Corruption to Chinese Stationariness*

JOHN STUART MILL, in his autobiography, wrote of his own intellectual career largely in terms of assimilation. It was a form of modesty, perhaps, but it also had its own kind of arrogance: the presentation of the author as microcosm. His education by his father was education into a system, having, as its chief components, utilitarian ethics, association psychology, Political Economy, and a theory of politics deductive in method and radical in prescription. His subsequent self-education, as he describes it, following his mental crisis, is an education in eclecticism: French and German more than English, Romantic as well as Positivist, Coleridgian as well as Benthamite. Historical relativism and the idea of progress, the value of the emotions, self-development, and diversity of experience, Wordsworth and Byron, Goethe and Humboldt, Saint-Simon and Comte, Coleridge and F D Maurice are all swept under the general rubric of 'many-sidedness', into a cultural *mélange* called 'the nineteenth century' In this way his life becomes a compendium of the cultural history of the age, the representative intellectual pilgrimage of nineteenth-century man. Of course, he would not have claimed that he was entirely undiscriminating. Eclecticism had limits, and assimilation was not promiscuity Kantian Idealist metaphysics was unassimilable; a fundamentally positivist epistemology was one component of the parental creed he never attempted to shed. His related belief in the validity of association psychology he stubbornly refused to abandon at the behest of Comte, though he conceded it needed completing by social science.

This much everyone who knows Mill knows, and it certainly seems enough to be going on with. Yet there is at least one cultural tradition which Mill did not so much reject as simply ignore, except in one specific respect, in his father's debate with Macaulay It is what we may here conveniently abbreviate to

Whiggism, which features in Mill's version neither of the eighteenth nor the nineteenth century It is an absence which notoriously includes the Scottish Enlightenment, despite his early reading, as well as, more predictably, Burke. To suggest, then, that a good deal in Mill's writings is consonant with longstanding Whig ideas and concerns runs, we have to allow, very much counter to his own sense of himself and of his intellectual heritage. In the last lecture, using examples from Mill's early essay on 'Civilization' and from *On Liberty*, I attempted to draw parallels chiefly between his individualism and the 'Country' and republican Whig ethics of civic virtue. Here, though Mill's historical anxiety and even pessimism forms a common background and will call for some unavoidable repetition, we shall be concerned more directly with politics; not with the individual, but with institutions and social forces, and hence with broad notions of Whig constitutionalism compared with the apprehensive liberalism of Mill's *Considerations on Representative Government*.

We may begin by looking at chapter five of the latter and setting it beside his father's famous controversy with Macaulay in the *Edinburgh* and *Westminster Reviews* over thirty years earlier It is true that, in his account of that controversy in his autobiography, Mill, while rebuking both parties, in his usual would-be eclectic fashion, for seeing only a part of the truth, seems to lean perhaps more to Macaulay's side of the case. But he does so only on methodological, not on substantive political grounds; he sees partial merit, that is, in Macaulay's inductivism compared with his father's deductive 'geometric' method, but he does not discuss in any detail the political issues they argue about, except to say that 'Identity of interest between the governing body and the community at large, is not, in any practical sense which can be attached to it, the only thing on which good government depends, neither can this identity of interest be secured by the mere conditions of election.'[1] In fact, Macaulay, while acknowledging that he offered no general theory of government himself, had made a powerful defence of the classic Whig notion of a balance of powers in the constitution, as against the adoption of manhood suffrage, as

---

[1] J. S. Mill, *Autobiography*, ed. J. Stillinger (Oxford University Press, 1971), 95.

the guardian of political liberty and continued progress. It is true that he does not offer it as a panacea and that he also lays much stress, in Humean fashion, on the influence of manners and opinion in controlling the appetites of men, as well as on the machinery of the constitution. Constitutions are not everything, but they are useful: 'Constitutions are in politics what paper money is in commerce. They afford great facilities and conveniences. But they are not power, but symbols of power, and will, in an emergency, prove altogether useless unless the power for which they stand be forthcoming.'[2] Constitutional machinery, in other words, will only work and only endure if it represents the real social forces of the day

In this form the traditional Whig theory of a constitutional balance was still available, alive, and usable in the 1820s and 1830s, and could be set polemically against utilitarian individualism. The latter, like the other form of the radical individualist argument, the doctrine of universal rights of man, issued naturally in demands for the representation in Parliament not of large collective social interests but of every man through his possession of the franchise.

With this contrast in mind we can turn back to J. S. Mill's *Considerations on Representative Government*, published in 1861, written, as we know, from a perspective which, under the tutelage of Tocqueville, tends to see the further advance of democracy, both in manners and in politics, as inevitable, and which also sees in it dangers to the liberal value of individuality Mill in *On Liberty* tells us that 'The circumstances which surround different classes and individuals, and shape their characters, are daily becoming more assimilated', and

As the various social eminences which enabled persons entrenched on them to disregard the opinion of the multitude, gradually become levelled; as the very idea of resisting the will of the public, when it is positively known that they have a will, disappears more and more from the minds of practical politicians; there ceases to be any social support for nonconformity—any substantive power in society, which, itself opposed to the ascendancy of numbers, is interested

---

[2] Macaulay, in Jack Lively and John Rees, *Utilitarian Logic and Politics: James Mill's 'Essay on Government' and Macaulay's Critique and the Ensuing Debate* (Oxford University Press, 1978), 207

in taking under its protection opinions and tendencies at variance with those of the public.³

The course of progress hitherto—though Mill does not quite see it like this—seems to have ended in a self-stultifying paradox. Individualism, by levelling traditional social distinctions and modes of power and influence, has become 'the ascendancy of numbers', and threatens individuality The man who so powerfully feels and asserts this view, as Mill does, is clearly attracted to a conception of a balanced representation of substantial social interests, not the supremacy of majorities of individuals, as the most congenial, if not perhaps the most readily available and realistic, form of political organization.

It is possible to read the eighteenth-century flavour of much of Mill's *Representative Government* in two ways; either as a sign of how little had changed in the empirical science of politics, as distinct from political philosophy, since the eighteenth century, or as an indication that dismay at the prospect of democracy naturally made the reflections of liberal thinkers sound more Whiggish. Both are relevant. For though there are obvious distinctively nineteenth-century references and sentiments in Mill's essay, particularly his emphasis on political education, there is certainly much in the lessons it tries to impart which would have been regarded as sound, if not particularly original, a hundred years earlier There is the same anxiety for liberty and the same sense that current social changes place it in jeopardy There are the same moralizing references to public spirit as indispensable to a free people, and the same admonitions against preferring selfish private interests to public ones. When Mill refers to the pessimism of the classical writers, their belief in life as an incessant struggle against deterioration, which we know had so influenced eighteenth-century notions of corruption and decay, he does so with an ostensible repudiation which in fact is virtually an endorsement: 'Though we no longer hold this opinion    believing that the tendency of things, on the whole, is towards improvement; we ought not to forget, that

---

³ *On Liberty*, in *The Collected Works of John Stuart Mill*, ed. J. M. Robson (Toronto, 1977), xviii. 275.

there is an incessant and ever-flowing current of human affairs towards the worse.'⁴

It is, however, in chapters four and five that Mill sounds most like an eighteenth-century Country Whig, brooding on the dangers to the balance of the constitution: from an encroaching executive tyrant, from factions which threaten to engross the powers of government and hence turn it into an oligarchy, and from the power of mere numbers. Whole sentences and paragraphs could easily pass as some eighteenth-century denunciations of growing executive power, supported by corrupted placemen; of the influence of faction, and of the erosion of public spirit by private interest. To take just one summarizing sentence from many· 'If the executive is weak, the country is distracted by mere struggles for place; if strong, it makes itself despotic, at the cheap price of appeasing the representatives by a share of the spoil.'⁵ These remarks are set by Mill in a historical frame: he is giving the lessons of history, and there are a number of historical references, particularly to France (place-hunting is the vice of the French, not the English). But they express, of course, the classic eighteenth-century anxieties necessarily always present concerning a constitution thought of as a delicate balance. And when, in chapter five, he turns directly to England, we find Macaulay's argument against James Mill echoed, probably not consciously, almost word for word. Why do the several powers in the constitution not abuse their power to overwhelm the others? It is because of 'The unwritten maxims of the Constitution—in other words, the positive political morality of the country' ⁶ Echoing Macaulay again, Mill argues that we cannot *rely* on a mass electorate to show the rationality to prefer long-term to short-term interest. His conclusion, the necessity for a balanced representation of what he calls 'a fair sample of every grade of intellect among the people which is at all entitled to a voice in public affairs' and the desirability of a representation 'equally balanced', so that 'no class, and no combination of classes likely to combine, should be able to exercise a preponderant influence in the government'⁷—all

---

⁴ *Considerations on Representative Government*, in *Collected Works*, xix. 388.
⁵ Ibid. 414.  ⁶ Ibid. 422.  ⁷ Ibid. 433, 446, 447

this, of course, is purest Whiggery, with no vestige left of James Mill's rejection of balance in favour of an all-out gamble on the rationality with which the majority would pursue its interest.

But it is time to start considering the differences between Mill and the Country Whig. And of course they lie not in the argument for a balance of forces, but in the identifications of the forces which need balancing. Mill speaks in the language of his time and of his own preoccupations when he speaks of the representation of 'every grade of intellect', the *Edinburgh* Reviewers also spoke in this vein. Again, Mill speaks of a balance of classes where an old-fashioned Whig would have spoken of estates or orders, and a more modern one, following Burke, would have spoken of great social interests. And he speaks too the language of the nineteenth-century progressive rather than the Country Whig when he speaks of a balance of forces as being necessary not just to liberty but to a further good of which liberty in turn is the precondition, namely 'progress'

> No community has ever long continued progressive, but while a conflict was going on between the strongest power in the community and some rival power; between the spiritual and temporal authorities; the military or territorial and the industrious classes; the king and the people, the orthodox, and religious reformers. When the victory on either side was so complete as to put an end to the strife, and no other conflict took its place, first stagnation followed, and then decay [8]

But in a democracy (and here we have pure Tocqueville) the difficulty is to find a 'social support, a *point d'appui*, for individual resistance to the tendencies of the ruling power' [9] The tendency of democracy to level 'social eminences' deprives minorities of their support in the multiplicity of rival powers and institutions. Here it seems we have a classic instance of a characteristic transformation. An essentially static eighteenth-century conception of an ideal mixture or balance of powers— a notion going back to Polybius—producing a unique point of balance, at which alone liberty is possible in the face of the

---

[8] *Considerations on Representative Government*, 459    [9] Ibid.

tendency of all earthly things to degenerate and decay, has given way to a characteristically nineteenth-century dynamic and optimistic conception, that of progress, of which the creative tension between contending forces is a necessary condition.

There is certainly such a contrast, and the nemesis which is the result of failure to maintain the tension in balance is correspondingly different in each case. To the Country Whig it is corruption and loss of liberty, the forfeiture of the free constitution, as the Romans had lost theirs, and with it their virtue and their greatness. To Mill it is the failure of the progressive impulse: stagnation, 'Chinese stationariness' The contrast holds very neatly so long as we make it, as we have done hitherto, with the Country Whig. But there was, of course, much more to eighteenth-century political thinking than neo-classical pessimism. It included very notably, particularly in the latter part of the century, notions of 'improvement' and 'the progress of society' It would not be surprising to find that Mill's conception here of progress through variety is an eighteenth-century one, if not, in his case, by origin, then certainly by anticipation. But before casting our net in the eighteenth century rather wider, we should perhaps cast it a little wider in the mid-nineteenth century also, to show that Mill's anxieties, and even up to a point Mill's ways of putting them, were by no means unique to himself or a mere eccentricity We may choose to think them misguided or irrelevant, but they were certainly not unusual. It has been convenient to illustrate our theme in some detail from Mill, but, of course, this was not intended to isolate him from his contemporaries. There are two other examples from the 1860s we might helpfully consider, because they present both close parallels to and interesting differences from Mill—Sir Henry Maine and Walter Bagehot: Maine, who published his first and most famous work, *Ancient Law*, in the same year as Mill's *Representative Government* (1861), and Bagehot, whose two most substantial works, *The English Constitution* and *Physics and Politics*, came out later in the decade.

In Maine and Bagehot, both twenty years younger than Mill, we find an element which in Mill is largely missing: it is a new sense of time, of the relation of the past to the present which makes the latter only a tiny fragment. The time-scale for the generation which came to intellectual maturity in the 1850s and 1860s was different; not merely longer but immensely longer In Maine it has something to do with comparative philology, which seemed to link the cultural history of Europe, in a remote past, with that of ancient India.[10] In Bagehot, by the mid-1860s, it is related explicitly to the most obvious source of all, Darwinism. Darwinian evolution is usually thought of as reinforcing, and providing new formulae for, the concept of progress. Yet we should appreciate, perhaps, that it could also have something like the reverse effect, of reinforcing anxiety, producing a sense of the extreme rarity and slowness of progressive movement, and of the precariousness of the particular circumstances on which, at any given moment, it depended. In Darwinian evolution, after all, not only do many species become extinct, but, though Darwin's contemporaries admittedly quite often ignored this, by far the greatest proportion of mutations are unsuccessful in establishing themselves; in most particular cases nature represses variety

For Mill, writing for the most part in the imaginative world of the older time-scale, the crucial historical transition was the same as for the writers of Scottish Enlightenment, though his language and immediate sources (chiefly Tocqueville, Guizot, and Saint-Simon) were different: it is the transition from feudalism to modernity Indeed, though Mill speaks freely of savages and barbarians, his focus of historical attention is really more contracted than that of his predecessors. Maine and Bagehot, by contrast, widen the perspective again, this time in a vocabulary coloured by geology and Darwinism, to a conjectural history of mankind, in Bagehot's case avowedly, and in Maine's with reservations which need not concern us now [11] In doing so, what chiefly impressed both of them was the awful, rock-like immobility of most of human society for most of its history For both of them modern progressive individualism was only a fragment of human history, a precarious experiment. Maine was powerfully impressed by oriental stationariness, seen, for once, at first hand:

[10] John Burrow, *Evolution and Society* (Cambridge University Press, 1966), 149–53. [11] Ibid. 161–4.

it is most difficult for a citizen of Western Europe to bring thoroughly home to himself the truth that the civilisation which surrounds him is a rare exception in the history of the world. The tone of thought common among us would be materially affected if we had vividly before us the relation of the progressive races to the totality of human life.[12]

It was to be an abiding preoccupation; a quarter of a century later he was summarizing it epigrammatically· 'the immobility of society is to the rule, its mobility is the exception.'[13] It followed that the conditions for that exception must be rare and seldom satisfied.

Bagehot too had a strong sense of their rarity, and of the immense immobilizing power of custom. Maine was an important influence on *Physics and Politics*,[14] though Bagehot gives custom an important function, while in Maine it usually provokes more unmixed irritation. The condition of progress, we are reminded in *Physics and Politics*, and also in many other places in Bagehot's writings, is an extraordinarily subtle balance between innovation and habit, between the necessary stabilizing force of custom and prejudice and a furtive or ingratiating originality Too much of the former, and society rested in what was in a sense its natural state of immobility, too much of the latter — as in the chattering, politically overheated society of France — and it broke into fragments and would have to be brought back into cohesion by a mechanically and violently imposed, despotic, and stultifying kind of order [15] Again we meet the crucial concept of balance, clothed, in *Physics and Politics*, in the new theoretical languages of Darwinism and neurophysiology Bagehot cherished what he thought of as rational progressive innovation, but he was anything but radical or impatient; he had an anxious, protective attitude to it, as to a frail plant.

We seem here in Bagehot to have something like an

[12] Henry Maine, *Ancient Law* (1861, 16th edn., London, 1897), 22.
[13] Humphrey Ward (ed.), *The Reign of Queen Victoria*, 2 vols. (London, 1887), i. 170.
[14] His name appears six times in the index, and there are other places also where he appears to have been drawn on.
[15] e.g. 'Letters on the French *Coup d'État* of 1851', in *The Collected Works of Walter Bagehot*, ed. Norman St John-Stevas, 15 vols. (London, 1965-86), iv 29-84; and 'Caesarism as it Now Exists', ibid. iii. 111-16.

evolutionist variation—only a few mutations 'take' and maintain themselves—of the old, Polybian, Whig notion of an oscillation between the despotic power of a tyrant and the licence of an excess of democracy Only the balance of a free mixed constitution offered relief, but it must necessarily always be precarious; the least tilting of the balance either way is sufficient to bring about again the unhappy alternative of despotism or licence. Again, as with Mill, we seem to have a modification of the notion of balance as the condition of liberty, with all its associated anxieties, converted into a necessary condition of the newer notion of progress and the avoidance, if possible, of stagnation and perhaps ultimate degeneration.

Yet though Bagehot's evolutionist idioms are novelties, the intellectual distance from the eighteenth century is greater in Maine; not because he was a believer in progress, as Bagehot was also, but because, of the two, he was more of a radical nineteenth-century individualist. Maine lived longer than Bagehot; long enough to see the Third Reform Act and the growth of what he called 'socialism' This for him was putting progress into reverse. He had expressed his notion of progress in a famous formula: the movement of the progressive societies is from status to contract. Progress is the emergence of individualism, of the free individual, from the kin-group, and then from serfdom; its accompanying movement in property-holding was from the initial collective ownership of the village-community, through feudal tenures, to the modern form of outright untrammelled ownership of disposable property [16] To revert to collective ownership and collective control over the individual would therefore, it seemed, be literally a reversal of progress.

Maine has no explanation of this except perversity and craven capitulation to democratic tendencies; he simply denounces it as 'unscientific' Because he was a more radical individualist than Bagehot, or even Mill under Tocqueville's guidance, he never squarely faced the paradox which they in

---

[16] John Burrow, 'The Village Community and the Uses of History', in N. McKendrick (ed.), *Historical Perspectives: Studies in English Thought and Society in Honour of J. H. Plumb* (London, 1974), 272-3.

some sense saw· that individualism may ultimately become the enemy of individuality For him, feudalism is not characterized by independent corporate and aristocratic powers; it is simply a stage in the process from collective to private ownership.[17] He seems to have had no clear sense of the feudal residues, the 'social eminences' which had allegedly mitigated the uniformity and individualism of the modern equality of citizenship. So when, in *Popular Government*, he wants to insist that progress comes essentially from aristocracies,[18] he blurs the distinction between the possible social functions of aristocracy and those of creative individuals: 'aristocracies' has no clear social meaning. Maine, in social terms, almost always sounds like an uninhibited mid-nineteenth-century individualist. Hence, despite his agitated political preference for balanced constitutions to pure sovereign democracies,[19] he has no clear answer to the dilemma that individualism, the simplification of all social relations to the rational one of free contract, seems to carry the corollary that in political terms each person is simply a unit. The obvious implication is ·a polity founded not on status but simply on numbers: manhood suffrage. He was, of course, by no means unusual in this among Victorian liberals—Robert Lowe would be another example—but Maine's case was complicated by the fact that he had large pretensions to understand the course of Western history considered as progress. But the movement towards democracy, which Mill had learnt from Tocqueville to regard as inevitable, left Maine merely fuming, and inclined to think of it just as an inexplicable irrationalism, a revival of the discredited metaphysical, Rousseauist doctrine of natural rights.[20]

Mill, by contrast, tried to think through the implications for individuality of the disappearance of what Tocqueville and he saw as feudal, aristocratic pluralism, a kind of social balance of counteracting powers. He tried, if not always very plausibly, to devise modern substitutes for the disappearing social eminences. In doing so he in a sense completed a long process

---

[17] Maine, *The Early History of Institutions* (London, 1875), 120, 126.
[18] Maine, *Popular Government* (2nd edn., London, 1886), 42.
[19] Ibid., esp. ch. iv.     [20] Ibid. 152.

by which property became first joined, and ultimately supplanted, by 'intellect' as the ground of political independence; the last constitutional survival, in the House of Commons, of the old notion of the representation of specific interests rather than numerically comparable constituencies was the university seats. Mill recognized, of course, that his unease at the 'tyranny of numbers', like his rejection of mere quantity of pleasure, set him at odds with his utilitarian heritage; he would presumably have been less pleased at the irony that makes it possible to recognize in his mature position the expiring effort of an aspect of the Whig tradition.

Bagehot more openly accepted the old Whig notion of the parliamentary representation of interests rather than numbers. Though he notoriously rejected as archaic the idea of a constitutional balance between king, lords, and commons, he had been anticipated in this by such good Whigs as Mackintosh and Jeffrey and even, by implication, by Paley and Burke, with the argument that the balance now lay *within* the House of Commons.[21] Bagehot continued to uphold a conception of balance in the latter sense; in the House of Commons all the great social interests should be represented and balanced and their conflicts mediated; it was essentially no different from Burke's conception.[22]

But there was a new vocabulary too, a modulation not just from 'estates' to the more realistic Burkian language of 'interests', but to the idiom and ways of thinking of a period inclined to think of itself as an age of individualism. For there were other possible individualisms than the utilitarian's 'every one to count for one' There was also the Romantic language of 'individuality' and its kindred terms we considered earlier, and one of these—the transposition of 'individuality', as it

---

[21] Winch, in Stefan Collini, Donald Winch, and John Burrow, *That Noble Science of Politics: A Study in Nineteenth-century Intellectual History* (Cambridge University Press, 1983), 56-7; M. J. C. Vile, *Constitutionalism and the Separation of Powers* (Oxford University Press, 1967), 216. The 18th-cent. notion of the representations of 'interests' in the Commons in a sense adumbrates this development; for Burke, see below, n. 43.

[22] e.g. Bagehot, *Works*, iii. 223-4. On Burke, see particularly J. R. Pole, *Political Representation in England and the Origins of the American Republic* (London, 1966), 444. I shall be much indebted in this lecture to Professor Pole's account of 18th-cent. concepts of representation. See below, n. 36.

were, into social terms—is another key word for Mill; and a pervasive concept, to which he tried to give a fashionable Darwinian gloss, for Bagehot: 'variety' Bagehot, like Mill, though more effectively and sympathetically, celebrated the diversity of individuals and human types, and their beneficial interaction in political life. It seems not an exaggeration to see, in Mill's notion of many-sidedness and exaltation of variety, and in Bagehot's celebration of the diversities of temperament and abilities found in *homo politicus*, the extension of older notions of balance, and of Parliament as the representation and harmonization of contending interests, to an increasingly mobile and self-consciously individualistic society, including eminences of merit and education, as well as of birth and property, and corporate and individual privilege.[23]

We have already considered aspects of this mutation and what analogies as well as distinctions it allows us to make between eighteenth- and nineteenth-century ideas. Here we need to suggest the possibility of a corresponding transition from balance to diversity, the former as a desired equilibrium in the face of an always encroaching corruption, the latter as the guarantee of continuing progress against a 'normal' yet dreaded condition of stasis, 'stationariness' But if we are not, in Mill's fashion, to overstate an antithesis between eighteenth- and nineteenth-century ways of thinking, we need, having made the initial contrast, to turn back to eighteenth-century ideas of progress, and to what may correspond in earlier periods, to mid-Victorian liberal notions of the social benefits of diversity

Initially, of course, when we look at the classical, Polybian idea of a mixed constitution, and at the eighteenth-century English version of it as a balance between king, lords, and commons, each acting as a check on the other, though the idea of liberty is central, the concept of progress seems very distant. The view of human political behaviour is bleak; the cherishing of liberty nervous. It is assumed in the classical theory that each of the pure forms of government tends to its characteristic type of corruption, monarchy to become tyranny, aristocracy

---

[23] I have elaborated on this point in Collini, Winch, and Burrow, *That Noble Science*, pp. 176-81.

to become oligarchy, democracy to become the rule of the mob. A mixed form of government is therefore best, but hard to hold in the necessary balance. It became axiomatic that any of the several components, given the chance to extend its powers at the expense of the others, would do so. In so far as there is a theory of history, it is cyclical, as in Polybius. The republican Whig Walter Moyle spoke typically, in his essay on the Roman government, of 'the natural transmigrations of dominion, from one form of government to another' and of 'the common circle in the generation and corruption of all states' [24] Men are instinctively and insatiably power-seeking, and will tend to abuse their power to rule in their own interests, to the full extent of their ability to do so. This, which makes the maintenance of a balance necessary, also makes it precarious. As another republican Whig, John Trenchard said, 'it is the Nature of Power to be ever encroaching' [25] Like the closely analogous eighteenth-century theory of a balance of power between states, it is a theory not of progress but of equilibrium. Metaphors from mechanics were inevitably drawn on, as in Blackstone's famous and highly complacent version of the theory [26] Trenchard combined mechanical and organic metaphors by making the latter, in the manner of Hobbes, only another form of mechanism: 'Government is political, as a human Body is natural, mechanism; both have proper Springs, Wheels and a peculiar Organisation     and when those Springs or Principle are destroyed by Accident or Violence, or are worn out by Time, they must suffer a natural or political Demise.'[27] The required tension between powers could hardly be maintained for ever, and metaphors of slacking and enervation are common. In the Machiavellian tradition which the English republican Whigs inherited through Harrington, it was seen as constantly necessary to check the process of decay by frequent restorations of the constitution to its original

---

[24] Caroline Robbins (ed.), *Two English Republican Tracts* (Cambridge University Press, 1969), 231.
[25] *Cato's Letters*, in D. L. Jacobson (ed.), *The English Libertarian Heritage* (Indianapolis, 1965), 257
[26] 'Like three distinct powers in mechanics, they jointly impel the machine of government in a direction different from what either acting by itself, would have done.' E. N. Williams (ed.), *The Eighteenth-century Constitution*, p. 75.
[27] *Cato's Letters*, p. 211.

principles—to quote Moyle again, 'by a thorough reformation of those corruptions and disorders, which length of time, a loose administration, and the depravity of human nature will introduce into the soundest and firmest constitutions of government'[28] Complacency was the privilege of supporters of the administration; to opponents it was obvious that the price of liberty was eternal vigilance and perhaps frequent restorations. The classic historical case of corruption and the loss of liberty was, of course, the fate of the Roman Republic. The example of Augustus, who had instituted an autocracy under the form of a republic, was one which spoke particularly eloquently to eighteenth-century Englishmen, because after the failure of the Stuarts, as they saw it, to subvert the mixed ancient constitution by force, the most likely threat was that of a covert executive tyranny insinuating itself gradually— insensibly, to use the eighteenth-century word—through corruption of Members of Parliament, while preserving all the outward forms of a parliamentary government, with first Walpole and then George III cast for the role of Augustus.[29]

So far we seem only to have confirmed our original contrast, of nineteenth-century 'progress' and eighteenth-century equilibrium; corruption and restoration, or a closed cycle of successive constitutional forms, seem the only kinds of historical momentum allowed for in the latter. Yet if we begin to attend further, not to the notion of 'balance' itself, but to the concept of that liberty which it is the function of balance to preserve, and even if we attend more closely to the supposed lessons of Roman history, we begin to find the contrast being replaced by a fundamental similarity and affinity with later, nineteenth-century notions of progress. For in the adaptation of the classical constitutional theories by Machiavelli, Montesquieu, and their English eighteenth-century followers, liberty itself is a dynamic force: liberty invigorates. In Machiavelli it makes republicans formidable in war, and leads to conquest, though conquest in turn comes to be seen, as in

---

[28] Robbins (ed.), *Two English Republican Tracts*, pp. 253-4.

[29] For the ambivalent connotations of 'Augustan', see H. Erskine Hill, *The Augustan Idea in English Literature* (London, 1983), ch. ix, and Howard D. Weinbrot, *Augustus Caesar in 'Augustan' England: The Decline of a Classical Norm* (Princeton, NJ, 1978).

Montesquieu's and Gibbon's versions of the decline of Rome, as a cause of luxury, despotism, and decline. In this there is therefore the tendency to see the operation of the dynamic force of liberty as creating the conditions of its own destruction. Yet in the celebrations of liberty as dynamic there is at least the potentiality of another view, particularly if success, 'opulence', can be detached, as increasingly came to be the case as the eighteenth century wore on, from the degenerative connotations of 'luxury'.[30] Consider how Trenchard's collaborator, Thomas Gordon, speaks of liberty in their series of *Cato's Letters*, in the 1720s. Liberty is celebrated as the source of every virtue, the nurse of trade, the parent of the arts and sciences, as well as of martial courage.[31] Liberty is what distinguishes men from sheep; it is the vital spring of self-moving energy in social life. Its opposite is slavery, to live at the will of another, and slavery too—political slavery, that is—has its social concomitants: stagnation and enervation.[32] 'From the Moment that the Romans lost their Liberty, their Spirit was gone', and 'when the Mind is enslaved by Fear and the Body by Chains, Inquiry and Study will be at an end'[33] Tyrants rule over a desert. And just as Rome is the historical paradigm of a once great but corrupted and degenerate state, so the paradigm case of political slavery is Turkey, or sometimes just more generally, 'Asiatic despotism' The notion of Asiatic despotism, in which everything derives from the will of a single man, was popularized by Montesquieu in the *Esprit des lois* as a distinct political category, to be set beside those of monarchy, aristocracy, and democracy, with their parallel corrupt versions, which go back to Aristotle. In the imputed characteristics of the Asiatic despotism—stagnation, sterility, absence of independent energy and free inquiry, a dead uniformity—as in the opposite ones of a state of liberty, we seem within touching distance already, in the first half of the

---

[30] Donald Winch, *Adam Smith's Politics: An Essay in Historiographic Revision* (Cambridge University Press, 1978), 37, 71-2.

[31] Pocock notes that the trading city offered a pattern of republican liberty alternative to that of Sparta and Rome, *Virtue, Commerce and History: Essays on Political Thought and History Chiefly in the Eighteenth Century* (Cambridge University Press, 1985), 249

[32] *Cato's Letters*, pp. 131-41.    [33] Ibid. 157, 189

eighteenth century, of the familiar nineteenth-century polarity with which we began: variety, diversity, progress, set against uniformity and stagnation, 'Chinese stationariness' Only the location for the latter, Turkish or Chinese, seems different, though Montesquieu does in fact speak of the static and uniform condition of China, as Hume does also.[34] The fundamental polarity on which Mill's warning rests is already present and powerful.

We have, therefore, two related eighteenth-century elements of which one, constitutional balance, is essentially static and even in a sense pessimistic, and the other, liberty, is dynamic. The two can coexist if the free constitution is seen as the necessary setting and, perhaps, inspiration for an energy which transcends the political sphere, exhibiting itself not just in conquest but in improvements in the arts and sciences. Even so, such improvements, like conquest, may be dangerous if they undermine the austerity on which liberty and energy alike depend.

But in the later eighteenth century the notion of 'balance' itself acquires a greater complexity, in ways which bring it closer to the nineteenth-century conception of 'diversity' That is, the notion of balance becomes less legalistic, more informal, ramifying, and pluralistic. The old notion of the House of Commons as one of the estates of the realm, an essential component of the vital balance, always entailed a certain complexity of interpretation, because it, unlike the other two houses, was a *representative* body. Representative of what? We were considering earlier the crucial notion of independence, in the republican Whig and Country Party view the indispensable quality of a member of˚ the House of Commons.[35] He was to be independent, above all, of course, of the Crown and its ministers, but what of the relation to those he represented?[36] The Country Party favoured shorter parliaments to keep the member from too much contamination by the specialized and corrupt world of ministerial politics,

---

[34] *Spirit of the Laws*, I. 298, 301, Hume, *Essays Moral, Political and Literary*, ed. T H. Green and T H. Grose, 2 vols. (London, 1875), I. 183.
[35] Above, ch. 4 n. 37
[36] For what follows I am heavily indebted to Pole, *Political Representation in England*, esp. 391 ff.

to restore him, so to speak, regularly to those he represented, but it generally stopped short of a theory of delegation, because the Country Party view emphasized or assumed the homogeneity of the 'popular' part of the constitution; 'interests' tended to be contrasted with virtue, and disapproved of as faction. The most generally accepted and respectable view of the MP's duty, and it remained so in the nineteenth century, seems to have been that the member should know the needs and grievances of his constituents but should himself be the final judge of the appropriate measures to meet them.[37] But what was being represented still needed specifying; it became increasingly clear that the Harringtonian identification of the popular part of the constitution with the landed freeholder was inadequate in a more prosperous, complex, educated society The notion of representation, in a sense, required a theory of society in order to explain what was represented, while the increasing radical attacks, towards the end of the century, on the allegedly unrepresentative character of the House of Commons, demanded a reply from the Establishment Whig.[38] The classic formulation was Burke's defence of the representation, not of individuals, as the theory of the rights of man required, which in effect would mean that force of numbers would always prevail, but of the great social interests, landed and commercial, the professions, the numerous collective interests of a complex society These interests required representing and harmonizing in a way that a Parliament elected by simple majority of numbers would not do. That would be to destroy the balance. But in fact it scarcely mattered whether one had the vote or not—if the representation of interests was comprehensive, one's interest would be sure to be represented somewhere, by somebody The lack of a uniform franchise-qualification was actually an advantage, preserving the diversity necessary to ensure the adequate representation of all important interests. In this way the theory of balance was shifted from the estates of the realm to the great interests to be found in society and represented in the House of Commons.[39] And increasingly, as we have

---

[37] Pole, *Political Representation in England*, e.g. 399, 411–12, 419
[38] Ibid. 442–4, 457–61.  [39] Ibid. 457

already seen, it was recognized that the old balance no longer existed.[40] The House of Commons was increasingly seen as sovereign, but this did not matter provided that a balance of interests was maintained within it.

The direct relevance of this to our general theme can now be put something like this: the theory of balanced estates was essentially static, except for the possibility of corruption, and the proper attitude to it was one of a strained, suspicious watchfulness, a sour jealousy of all signs of 'encroachment' The new theory of interests still required attentiveness—new interests might develop, which would require adequate representation; this was essentially the Whig view of the 1832 Reform Act. But because the new theory was a theory not directly of power-seeking, contending estates, but simply of a diversity of interests, that diversity itself could become a subject of celebration and wonder Instead of a tense though beneficial deadlock of contending forces, we have something, above all in the rhetoric of Burke, more like a symphonic diversity in unity, which it is the function of Parliament to harmonize. The appropriate attitude to it is therefore not just a jealous watchfulness; it is jubilation, and Burke is not just the legitimator of the representation of interests, he is its celebrator Burke speaks the language of balance and compromise no longer, as it were, grudgingly, or, like Blackstone, with a kind of aesthetic or quasi-devout appreciation of its mechanism, but as one rejoicing in the fecund diversity and energy of life itself: 'The nature of man is intricate; the objects of society are of the greatest possible complexity· and therefore no single disposition or direction of power can be suitable either to man's nature or to the quality of his affairs.'[41] If this is still in some sense the language of the mixed constitution, it is a remarkable creative elaboration of it.

In Burke's hands, then, what was initially a pessimistic theory of mechanical checks has turned into a celebration of harmonized diversity, the latter being seen as a richness desirable in itself. It seems hardly necessary to underline how

---

[40] Above, n. 21.
[41] 'Reflections on the Revolution in France', in *The Writings and Speeches of Edmund Burke*, 12 vols. (London, 1900), iii. 312.

far we have travelled towards Mill's and Bagehot's kind of progressive liberalism. The long-standing occidental–oriental contrast is present in Burke too, as also, more surprisingly perhaps in view of his celebrated defence of 'prejudice', is a conception of 'opinion' as potentially immobilizing and associated with stagnation, though no one would claim it was his leading thought, as it became Mill's. Contrasting the Indian caste-system with western flexibility, Burke said 'we have more versatility of character and manners. We know what the empire of opinion is in human nature  The variety of balanced opinions in our minds weakens the force of each.'[42] No one, I take it, could on internal grounds object to the attribution of such a remark to Mill, Bagehot, or Maine.

The conception we have been considering involves giving a positive value to each of the constituent elements harmonized in a free parliamentary system, and broadening the composition of those elements from an original legalism, which, formally at least, recognized only estates of the realm, to something like a tentative sociology of interests: 'a great official, a great professional, a great military and moral interest  has been gradually formed in the kingdom. These new interests must be let into a share in the representation, else possibly they may be inclined to destroy those institutions of which they are not permitted to partake.'[43] That is one possible line of development: the mutation of a watchful, constitutionalist concept of balance into a celebration of diversity and of the vitality and richness it promotes and expresses.

But there is another, not constitutional but historical and cultural, where the emphasis on diversity, rather than, more strictly speaking, balance, is present from the beginning. We can see it, for example, in Hume's essay on the progress of the arts, in the remarks on China we noted earlier. Hume's overall argument is that liberty is the parent of the arts, though it is under absolute governments they become most polished. One part of his argument almost recapitulates the one we have been considering: from balance to diversity and hence progress.

---

[42] Quoted in Gerald W Chapman, *Edmund Burke: The Practical Imagination* (Cambridge, Mass., 1967), 248.

[43] Burke, *Thoughts on the Cause of the Present Discontents* in *Writings and Speeches*, 1. 519

'To balance a large state or society is a work of so great difficulty that no human genius is able by the mere dint of reason and reflection, to effect it. The judgements of many must unite in this work.'[44] Flexibility, trial and error, are essential to the progress of arts and manufactures. Why have they not developed further in China? 'China is one vast empire, speaking one language, governed by one law, and sympathising in the same manners. The authority of any teacher, such as Confucius, was propagated easily from one corner of the empire to the other. None had the courage to resist the torrent of popular opinion.'[45] It is hard to believe Mill did not have this passage in mind when he compared modern public opinion and the Confucian bureaucracy

The contrast is with Greece: 'Where a number of neighbouring states have a great intercourse of arts and commerce, their mutual jealousy keeps them from receiving too lightly the law from each other The contagion of popular opinion spreads not so easily from one place to another.' After the establishment of the Roman Empire, the Catholic Church established uniformity, 'to the utter depravation of every kind of learning. But mankind, having at length thrown off this yoke Europe is at present a copy at large, of what Greece was formerly a pattern in initiative.'[46]

We find the same arguments echoed exactly in Gibbon. The occidental–oriental contrast becomes a more emphatic feature than in Hume's essay The antithesis of republican liberty and oriental despotism and servility is the most important single polarity around which the first half, at least, of Gibbon's history is organized. And even while the Roman Empire still enjoyed the remains of republican dignity and self-respect, the uniformity it imposed is seen as a weakness, sapping vitality and initiative: 'The minds of men were gradually reduced to the same level, the fire of genius was extinguished '[47] Gibbon's frequent adjective for the Roman provinces was 'servile', they had no independent spring of action, no liberty or individuality, and hence no initiative or energy And one

---

[44] Hume, *Essays*, I. 185.   [45] Ibid. 183.   [46] Ibid. 182–3.
[47] Edward Gibbon, *The History of the Decline and Fall of the Roman Empire*, ed. J. B. Bury, 7 vols. (6th edn., London, 1912), I. 56.

of the chief symptoms and causes of decay, particularly with the removal of the imperial capital to Byzantium, was what the nineteenth century would learn to call bureaucracy; the antithesis of the Whig mixed constitution and English traditions of local independence.

The distinctions of personal merit and influence, so conspicuous in a republic, so feeble and obscure under a monarchy, were abolished by the despotism of the emperors, who substituted in their room a severe subordination of rank and office, from the titled slaves who were seated on the steps of the throne, to the meanest instruments of arbitrary power.[48]

Byzantium, in Gibbon's presentation, became a type of oriental despotism, sterile and static; static because servile.

So far this may seem only a reiteration of the eighteenth-century commonplace we considered earlier· the connection between liberty and energy, despotism and lethargy, presented in terms of the familiar occidental-oriental antithesis. But Gibbon, repeating Hume, also makes room for specific endorsement of variety and diversity as well as of constitutional liberty Just as the Empire was enervated by its uniformity, so 'The cities of ancient Greece were cast in the happy mixture of union and independence, which is repeated on a larger scale, but in a looser form, by the nations of modern Europe.' Variety and emulation are invigorating, excesses mutually corrective.[49]

Arguably the chief transmitter to nineteenth-century English liberalism of the conception of the diversity of modern Europe as its distinctive characteristic and the source of its progress was Gibbon's French editor, Guizot, in whose hands it became an elaborated liberal philosophy of history In ancient civilizations we are struck by their uniformity· 'society has attached itself to a solitary dominant principle, which has determined its institutions, its customs, its creeds, in one word, all its developments.' By contrast, in modern Europe variety and struggle are everywhere: 'all principles of social organisation co-exist therein; powers spiritual and temporal; elements theocratic, monarchical, aristocratic, democratic; all

---

[48] Gibbons, *Decline and Fall*, ii. 159    [49] Ibid. vi. 108.

orders, all social arrangements mingle and press upon one another.'[50] This tension is the condition both of liberty and progress; it is the balance of power and the mixed constitution inflated into a cultural, sociological, intellectual, and historical liberalism. It is not surprising that J. S. Mill found Guizot congenial and instructive, as an authority for what was becoming one of his own central ideas: if any one power—clergy, kings, nobility, commercial aristocracy—had ever made itself supreme in Europe, stagnation would have ensued, as in 'the great stationary despotisms of the east'.[51] It is more surprising that Mill could apparently find in Gibbon nothing but 'a few generalities about despotism and immorality and luxury'.[52] Or rather it would be surprising if one did not know Mill. Guizot was doubly acceptable as nineteenth-century and French; one sometimes wonders if Mill ever re-read any eighteenth-century historian after the age of twelve.[53]

Guizot was widely read and cited as an authority on government and history among mid-Victorian liberals. He was particularly important to Freeman and to Thomas Hare, as well as to Mill.[54] But of course the French author and admirer of the English Whig political tradition whose influence overtopped even his was Tocqueville, because it was Tocqueville who made most persuasively available the lessons of the two societies with which nineteenth-century Whigs and Liberals were most concerned after their own, the United States and France. The United States became the paradigm case of oppressive democratic 'public opinion'. France had long been a model of despotism, and then, later, of the unhappy but seemingly inevitable alternation of despotism and democratic excess of which the Greek students of constitutions had spoken. As such, France, in the nineteenth century, took over for a

---

[50] François Guizot, *The History of Civilization, from the Fall of the Roman Empire to the French Revolution*, trans. William Hazlitt, 3 vols. (London, 1894), I. 22, 24.

[51] J. S. Mill, *Essays on French History and Historians*, in *Collected Works*, xx. 270.

[52] Ibid. 263.     [53] Mill, *Autobiography*, pp. 6, 7, 9

[54] Guizot is cited in Hare's *Election of Representatives* (London, 1859) almost as often as Burke. For Freeman's reading of Guizot, chiefly for his *History of Federal Government*, see W. R. M. Stephens, *The Life and Letters of Edward Freeman*, 2 vols. (London, 1895), I. 165, 171. Sismondi was also an influence.

while from Rome the role of protagonist in history's greatest cautionary tale. The occidental–oriental contrast retained its force, but 'Chinese stationariness' was never more than picturesque imagery It was France that offered the Whig or Liberal his favourite antithetical example, for purposes of warning or self-congratulation. But it was chiefly from Tocqueville that he learnt to read French history in a different, though no more genial or less relevant, way, as a story of a centuries-long process of bureaucratic centralization, running deep below the surface on which autocracy and democracy played out their dramas. For the British to learn from Tocqueville the importance of local initiative and decentralization was a little like M. Jourdain learning that he spoke prose, but there was a new self-consciousness about such things from the 1830s onwards, as reforming governments made (highly modest) inroads into matters which hitherto local communities had managed—or not managed—for themselves. And as invocations of the old palladium of English liberty at the centre of the national life, the balanced constitution, seemed, after 1867, an increasingly forlorn piece of Whig piety, so notions of the diffusion of power, and of the sustaining or creating of various kinds of corporate social eminences with which to confront the sovereign Parliament and State, came to seem increasingly appealing.

# 6
## Subordinate Partialities[1]
### Sinister Interests and Corporate Rights

THE routes we have followed so far have been chronological but not sequential. In each lecture I have attempted to tell a story from, roughly, the early or mid-eighteenth century to the 1860s and 1870s, or occasionally a little later. Taken together, therefore, the lectures have formed, not a sequence, but, apart from some inevitable straying and overlapping, a set of parallel lines. In this last lecture, however, the period will be chiefly the later nineteenth and early twentieth centuries, so that it will have something of the character of an epilogue. It seems appropriate, then, to begin with recapitulation.

I began by criticizing a view of the history of political thought in Britain in the eighteenth and nineteenth centuries which makes it virtually coextensive with the development of liberal individualism, represented by natural rights theories, Political Economy, Benthamite Utilitarianism, and Social Darwinism, and the challenges to it by a Tory paternalism, and, eventually, socialism. It is a picture which conveniently fits the central political preoccupations of our own day, troubled as we are by the issues of nationalization and 'privatization', and relatively less troubled, except in special circumstances like Northern Ireland, by constitutional issues, fundamental questions of sovereignty, representation, and the franchise. Even so, of course, the simple dichotomy of State versus individual, which first became central in English political thought in the later nineteenth century, hardly allows for the persisting vitality in such issues as the relations of central to local government, the constitutional role of the House of Lords, and the independence of such corporate bodies as the trades

---

[1] 'The love to the whole is not extinguished in this subordinate partiality.' Burke, *Reflections*, in *The Writings and Speeches of Edmund Burke*, 12 vols. (London, 1900), iii. 492.

unions, the Church of England, the BBC, or the universities. Many of the authors we have considered would have understood the paradox that an extreme individualism, in the sense of an insistence on the uniform, theoretical equality of all citizens and a corresponding disrespect for all institutions but the state (exemplified in Rousseau, and in the French Revolution's Law of Associations) can be combined with vigorous assertion and extension of the powers of government. It was a Whig cliché, most memorably asserted by Burke, that the extremes of democratic individualism and despotism meet.[2]

In the later nineteenth century, with manhood suffrage established, the notion of politics as the arena, above all, for the contest between what was called collectivism and individualism became for the first time paramount. Yet in the English political theory of the period the Whig tradition, as it is tempting to call it, did not succumb without articulate protest to this radical simplification, but rather took on new forms which seemed, for a while at least, appropriate to the kinds of complexity characteristic of a modern, rather than a landed, aristocratic society It is to these that I want to turn shortly

But to continue to recapitulate: in the second lecture I considered forms of eighteenth-century Whiggism which are not assimilable to contractarianism and doctrines of natural rights: neo-classical notions of liberty as public participation rather than the private enjoyment of rights; and then, subsequently, a conception of civilization as the spontaneous, unintended transformation and (for the most part) improvement of society and manners, which tended to make the relation of government to society one primarily of adjustment and mediation. In the last three lectures I have tried to consider some of the implications of a perceptible loss of confidence, among educated liberals, in the generally beneficial nature of that social transformation; it was an unease which focused chiefly, of course, on the notion of an inevitable

---

[2] ' if the present project of a republic should fail, all securities to a moderated freedom fail along with it, all the indirect restraints which mitigate despotism are removed' Ibid. 479 Cf. Gibbon on Byzantium, above, ch. 5 n. 48.

advance of democracy—seen not only as a type of government but as a system of manners, a form of social life—and on the role of the liberal intellectual within it. I tried to elaborate on what were thought of as the social, moral, and political preconditions of liberalism and progress: the influence of educated opinion; personal individuality and autonomy; and the social diversity expressed and protected by political arrangements which allowed for the adequate representation of diverse interests. And I have tried, allowing for contrasts and mutations, to show how these beliefs and assumptions may be related, by analogy or historical connection, to earlier, eighteenth-century Whig notions of enlightenment and improvement, of personal and economic independence and autonomy, of liberty as protected by a balance of forces, and of its beneficial effects: energy, initiative, and diversity

In all of this I have been treating the liberal theories and anxieties of the 1850s and 1860s, and particularly those of J. S. Mill, as a kind of climacteric, a culmination which is also an effort to restate and defend a Whig-Liberal position seen as crumbling before the onset of mass democracy and the tyranny of lower middle-class opinion. To present it in this way has been justified because that is how the authors we have chiefly attended to saw it themselves. Sometimes the anxieties of the 1860s and 1870s deepened in the 1890s, as in Lecky's *Democracy and Liberty* or C. H. Pearson's *National Life and Character* Even those further to the left, like Shaw and Wells, tended to see the advent of democracy in terms of apocalyptic crisis.

As always, hope, disillusionment, and despair were matters of generation and age as well as response to events. The younger generation of university liberals of the 1850s and 1860s, James Bryce, A. V Dicey, Leslie Stephen, and the other contributors to *Essays on Reform*, repudiated Whig timidity, tended to reject the old notions of interest-representation and constitutional balance as mechanical and unrealistic, and declared that they had no fear of numbers. They pinned their faith not on a balance of interests but on the diffusion of public virtue and political experience, and saw more of it in the skilled working class, trained in fraternity and co-operative action in the trade unions, than in the tradesmen and shopkeepers, the ten-pound householders of the 1832 Reform Act. 'Virtue' and 'interests', from the early eighteenth century onwards, tended to function as rivals and alternatives in political argument, the one being trusted as the other was less well-regarded.[3] Country Party theorists had called for public virtue and denounced 'faction', while Burke, later, had celebrated the multiplicity of interests and criticized the cult of an overstrained, impossibly exalted conception of patriotism and political virtue, developed from common neo-classical sources by Country Whigs and French Jacobins. But when the young authors of *Essays on Reform* became in due course disillusioned older men, disenchanted, as they mostly were, with the results of the urban working-class franchise they had called for, there was another generation of young liberal intellectuals, the spokesmen of the New Liberalism, L. T Hobhouse, J. A. Hobson, and others; apologists for the further measures of state intervention which Dicey anathematized as 'Collectivism', who nevertheless—Hobhouse in particular—continued to lay claim to the liberal heritage.

Yet in so far as the 1860s and 1870s see the emergence, for the first time, of something like a strain of liberal intellectual pessimism, a partial loss of that confidence in an advancing civilization which nineteenth-century progressive Whigs of the Edinburgh stamp had inherited from the Scottish Enlightenment, it does mark a kind of climacteric. To the extent that the long contest between moderate Whigs and radicals had corresponded to antagonistic views of political representation—the representation of interests being opposed by the representation of individuals—it was effectively ended. On this issue Price and Paine had been opposed by Burke; in the 1820s the Philosophic Radicalism of James Mill had been countered by Macaulay In the 1860s Bagehot restated the Whig case for interest representation through diversities of franchise;[4] in the 1890s Lecky mourned for it. But 1867 settled it; formally at least, numbers, and the kind of

---

[3] 'The advance of "interests" into the area of legitimized representation meant the decline of one force that had never been voted for: virtue.' J. R. Pole, *Political Representation in England and the Origins of the American Republic* (London, 1966), 531.

[4] Not only he, of course; cf. e.g. Earl Grey, *Parliamentary Government Considered with Reference to a Reform of Parliament* (London, 1858), 64–5.

individualism embodied in the doctrine of representation of persons, prevailed. And it was also, of course, the point at which the Whig party ceased to have an independent, effective existence. Individualism triumphed, yet only, in the minds of some pessimistic liberals, to reveal what I have called the paradox—which they did not quite see as such—that individualism might turn out to be the enemy of individuality by producing the kind of society in which the latter was stifled and a democratically elected Parliament dabbled in a collectivism which they saw as stopping the motor of social progress.

Is it the case, then, that any realistic attempt to trace connections of nineteenth- with eighteenth-century political thought in England ends here? Apart from a certain nostalgic Whiggism among older Liberals, often by now Liberal Unionists, is the only story to be told as the history of political thought one of debates over 'collectivism' between intransigent liberal-individualists like Maine, Dicey, Spencer, and the members of the Liberty and Property Defence League on the one hand, and New Liberals, Fabians, Marxists, and disciples of Henry George on the other? If so, then the supposed links with the eighteenth century, presumably most notably to Adam Smith's denunciation of mercantile monopolies and his 'system of natural liberty', can hardly be said to have been neglected; they have, rather, been vulgarized beyond historical recognition and there is no need to re-emphasize them.

But there is another, at the time highly acclaimed and influential, line of thought in which, under a modish, late nineteenth-century, metaphysical, and legal vocabulary, it is possible to see a continuation, not necessarily conscious, of long-standing Whig and mid-Victorian liberal ideas and concerns. It would hardly be too much to say that from 1900 to the 1920s, in the writings of many English academic political theorists, it seemed to point the way forward and to threaten to relegate the individualist/collectivist debate to the status of a late-Victorian brawl. Its central theme is the scope and powers of the state, but it is not concerned with what was called at the time 'socialism' and we have learnt to call welfare legislation, though it did emphatically involve the topical question—topical then and now—of the rights and privileges of trade unions. The theoretical discussion of the relation of the state to corporate bodies and voluntary associations of all kinds, which dominated British political thought in the early years of this century, has left relatively little intellectual residue, and certainly none commensurate with its importance at the time. The predictions of its exponents have, in that respect, been falsified. Historians of political thought have given their attention to it, under what has become its most familiar general description, as 'Political Pluralism', but it remains a historical episode rather than a living influence. Here I am concerned primarily with the analogies it exhibits with earlier forms of Whiggism and liberalism; analogies such that its demise can represent, if perhaps only temporarily, a kind of closure.

Apart from its historically circumscribed, though at the time widely ramifying character, which makes it appropriate to speak of it as an episode, its most obvious feature is the way it cut across the lines of party As a theory which purported to limit the claims of the state, it had an appeal to conservatives, liberals, syndicalists, and even some kinds of anarchist. In affirming the corporate personality and rights of churches, joint-stock companies, and trade unions, it transcended—or seemed to offer to do so—the division of political theories into left and right. To get a sense of its contemporary prominence we might consider for a moment, for example, the short history of modern English political thought published in 1915 by Ernest Barker Barker, who was a moderate sympathizer, spoke of it, at least partially, in the language of endorsement, as an important and, so far as it went, justified critique of utilitarian individualism.

If we are individualists now, we are corporate individualists. Our 'individuals' are becoming groups. No longer do we write *The Man versus the State*; we write '*The Group versus the State*' There is much talk of federalism in these days. Behind the talk lies a feeling that the single unitary State, with its single sovereignty, is a dubious conception, which is hardly true to the facts of life. Every State, we feel, is something of a federal society, and contains within its borders different national groups, different churches, different economic organisations, each exercising its measure of control over its members. This federalistic feeling is curiously widespread.[5]

[5] Ernest Barker, *Political Thought in England from Herbert Spencer to the Present Day* (London, 1915), 181.

Barker goes on to instance Guild Socialism ('The newest Socialism has abandoned the paths of a unitary collectivism managed from a single centre') and also the sympathy towards ideas of devolution for Ireland, Wales, and Scotland in the new Liberalism.

A theory of the corporate personality of groups had a good deal of relevance when the law on trade unions was in a confused state: the Taff Vale judgment, making them collectively responsible for the acts of their agents, seeming to treat them as endowed with full legal personality, while the Osborne judgment implied the reverse. The rights of churches to behave as fully corporate bodies had been brought into prominence by the House of Lords decision in the Free Church of Scotland case, while a theory which endorsed the autonomy of corporate life appealed to High Anglicans who, in the previous three-quarters of a century, had lost so many of the privileges of an establishment, yet whose church was subject to the sovereignty of a Parliament in which Dissenters, Jews, and atheists now sat.

The most comprehensive statement of the theory of association, in fact, was provided by J. N. Figgis, in his influential *Churches and the Modern State* (1913), to which both Harold Laski and G. D H. Cole acknowledged a debt. But behind Figgis there were the two men to whom he acknowledged his own discipleship; both Cambridge historians, though of different types and interests—Maitland and Acton.[6] It is in them that we see most clearly the connections of pluralism with the anxieties of mid-Victorian liberalism: worries about the rights and influence of minorities, fears for the preservation of social diversity, and independent energy in the face of a levelling society and an encroaching democratic state.

In Acton, unlike Maitland, the links with English Whiggism, particularly Burke, are explicit; he is also, it seems, more

---

[6] Three, if one includes Creighton. Figgis's acknowledgement to Maitland for the central theoretical ideas of *Churches and the Modern State* (London, 1913) is explicit; see p. x. Acton's influence is more diffuse but there must have been much that Figgis, who edited his lectures after his death, found congenial. For Cole and Laski, see e.g. G. D. H. Cole, *Social Theory* (London, 1920), 10, 11, Herbert Deane, *The Political Ideas of Harold J. Laski* (New York, 1955), 5, 13. There is a good survey of the Pluralist episode in Rodney Barker, *Political Ideas in Modern Britain* (London, 1978); see also David Nicholls, *Three Varieties of Pluralism* (London, 1975).

crucially influenced by Tocqueville. His interests are sometimes differently focused too: on federalism, and on the position of national minorities in a multinational state. Federalism, of course, was placed on the political agenda of later nineteenth-century Britain by the development of the self-governing colonies, the persistence of Irish discontent, and the consequent proposals to save the unity of the Empire by schemes of imperial federation. The problem can be seen, in a broad sense, as similar to the Whig's problem of the early nineteenth century· how to adjust traditional constitutional arrangements to an advancing civilization and the emergence of new and articulate interests. In that sense imperial federation was the Fourth Reform Act that was never enacted.

But Acton was not identified with the imperial cause, as his predecessor in the chair of history at Cambridge, Seeley, so pre-eminently was. His endorsement of federalism, like Freeman's, was of a more distinctively liberal kind. The distinction between Acton and Freeman, however, is that between the Whig and the Liberal democrat. For Freeman, writing in high liberal-democratic optimism in the mid-century, federalism, along with a vigorous system of local government, offered the only prospect, under modern conditions, of re-creating the political life, the energetic political participation, available to the free citizen of the ancient *polis*.[7] Acton's approval anxiously echoed the Whiggish endorsement of diversity of powers and opinions we have seen in Gibbon and J. S. Mill. Federalism was praised as 'the best check on democracy By multiplying centres of government and discussion it promotes the diffusion of political knowledge and the maintenance of healthy and independent opinion.'[8]

In the same spirit Acton provided a Whiggish defence of the Catholic Church, part of whose function was 'To maintain the necessary immunity in one supreme sphere, to reduce all political authority within defined limits' [9] It is a defence which reminds us of Guizot's approval of the plurality of powers;

---

[7] E. A. Freeman, *History of Federal Government in Greece and Italy* (1863; 2nd edn., London, 1893), 69, 156.
[8] 'The History of Freedom in Antiquity' (1877), in Lord Acton, *The History of Freedom and Other Essays*, introd. J. N. Figgis (London, 1909), 20.
[9] Ibid. 29

in the later nineteenth century in Europe, in the period of the *Kulturkampf* in Bismarck's Germany and the expulsion of the religious orders from France, it had a sharp topicality But for the Church, Acton said—clearly looking for variations on a familiar theme—'Europe would have sunk into a Byzantine or Muscovite despotism' [10]

'Immunity' and 'supreme', in these two words, in his account of the Church's function, we have the two sides of Acton's Whiggish liberalism or his liberal Whiggism, the institutional and the ideological. Acton was in many ways a Whig, but he was not exactly an English Whig historian of the type of Stubbs and Freeman; his scale was European, and he was interested in the history of ideas rather than institutions, and above all in what was for him the supreme idea, the sovereignty of conscience. In his essays on the history of freedom we can see the dim outlines of the great history of liberty he never wrote: it would have had to contain both elements, the diffusion of power and the idea of liberty as freedom of conscience. He obviously had some difficulty in combining them, and it sometimes led him to be ironical at the expense of the Whig enthusiasm for the barbarian liberty inherited from the German woods.[11] Aquinas and Suarez were more congenial. It was in Acton's version of the Church, above all, that the two strands came together: both an institution among others, an independent power in the European commonwealth of contending forces, and also the unique vehicle for the preservation and transmission of the supreme spiritual idea of freedom. It was thus both an 'immunity' in the medieval sense, and the institutional guardian of the 'supreme' interest of mankind.

Federalism, diffusion of power, and the role of the church as the palladium of spiritual and hence political freedom are linked, for example, in Acton's version of the French Revolution. The French Revolutionaries 'armed themselves

---

[10] 'The History of Freedom in Christianity' (1877), ibid. 35.

[11] Most famously in his Cambridge Inaugural Lecture: 'A speech of Antigone, a single sentence of Socrates, a few lines that were inscribed on an Indian rock before the second Punic War, the footsteps of a silent yet prophetic people who dwelt by the Dead Sea, and perished in the fall of Jerusalem, come nearer to our lives than the ancestral wisdom of barbarians who fed their swine on the Hercynian acorns.' Lord Acton, *Lectures on Modern History* (London, 1906), 3.

with power to crush every adverse, every independent force, and especially to put down the Church, in whose cause the provinces had risen against the capital. They met the centrifugal federalism of the friends of the Gironde by the most resolute centralization.'[12] France becomes, in the nineteenth century, the chief example of a centralized plebiscitary autocracy And modern liberal nationalism in Europe derives its impetus from France, not from England: 'The substance of the idea of 1789 is not the limitation of the sovereign power, but the abrogation of intermediate powers    If liberty were its object its means would be the establishment of great independent authorities not derived from the State    but its object is equality ' In a sketch of nineteenth-century Europe Acton contrasts English and French concepts of nationality  The former is historic, traditionalist, in effect, Whig: 'it tends to diversity and not to uniformity, to harmony and not to unity ' The latter is Rousseauist and utopian, 'founded on the perpetual supremacy of the collective will, of which the unity of the nation is the necessary condition, to which every other influence must defer, and against which no obligation enjoys authority, and all resistance is tyrannical' [13]

Acton's account of nationalism concludes with a defence of the multi-national state, which is an extension of the arguments for diversity we have seen in Gibbon, Burke, Guizot, and Mill, to cover the case of national minorities. Acton, in fact, here reverses something like a liberal cliché, found in Freeman and Mill, that only in a homogeneous nation are free institutions possible;[14] Mill, indeed, considered the issue of national minorities briefly at the end of *Representative Government*, but with a strong predisposition against provincial backwardness and narrow-mindedness, epitomized in the Breton left 'to sulk on his own rocks' [15] But to Acton diversity of nations under the same sovereignty ensures diversity of

---

[12] 'Sir Erskine May's "Democracy in Europe"' (*Quarterly Review*, 1878), in *The History of Freedom*, p. 88.
[13] 'Nationality' (1862), ibid. 280, 288.
[14] Freeman, 'The Physical and Political Bases of National Unity', in A. S. White (ed.), *Britannic Confederation* (London, 1892). J. S. Mill: 'Free institutions are next to impossible in a country made up of different nationalities', *Representative Government*, in *Collected Works*, xix. 547     [15] Ibid. 549

opinion, and, in an exaggerated version of Mill's kind of anxiety, nation-states are said to be inherently stagnant: 'Where political and national boundaries coincide, society ceases to advance.'[16] Earlier he has presented the multinational state as a transposed case of a Burkian constitution, concluding with a neat assertion of the independence of society from polity·

It provides against the servility which flourishes under the shadow of a single authority by balancing interests, multiplying associations, and giving to the subject the restraint and support of a combined opinion   This diversity in the same State is a firm barrier against the intrusion of government beyond the political sphere which is common to all into the social department which escapes legislation and is ruled by spontaneous laws.[17]

The other of Figgis's mentors, Maitland, had no particular interest in national minorities or federalism. As a lawyer his concern was with institutions, though as a pagan liberal, with a marked vein of anticlericalism, he had no tenderness to churches as such. Yet as the chief English proponent of the theory of associations he was certainly the more direct and specific influence on Figgis's *Churches and the Modern State*. The *locus classicus* is, of course, Maitland's immensely influential preface to his translation of Otto von Gierke's *Political Theories of the Middle Ages*, published in 1900  Gierke's work presented a metaphysical-legal theory of the real personality of the group, the *Genossenschaft*. Maitland called it the greatest book he had ever read. The German theory of the legal corporation had fascinated him for a number of years. It provided him with what he felt to be an indispensable conceptual tool for interpreting the legal conceptions found in medieval documents, and it gave a strong impress to a number of his writings, notably *Township and Borough*, and several important papers. It also helped to give him a marked sympathy with contemporary forms of spontaneous association when they found difficulty in asserting claims to full legal status and hence to the enjoyment of corporate rights.

That Maitland came to see group life, and through it a general conception of modern society, essentially in terms of

[16] Acton, 'Nationality', in *History of Freedom*, p. 290.
[17] Ibid. 289-90.

the German juristic language he derived, above all, from
Gierke, is indisputable. It was the vital inspiration. So far,
therefore, he may seem to offer unpromising material for an
attempt to link him to indigenous traditions of political thinking
to which, unlike Acton, he generally seems indifferent. Even more
than chapter three of Mill's *On Liberty*, Maitland's introduction
to Gierke, and crucial essays like 'Moral Personality and Legal
Personality', seem to be immediately, and in Maitland's case
almost exclusively, referable to a German source. Yet, as with
Mill's essay, of course, we can ask questions about the native
assumptions and traditions which made the foreign ideas
congenial. There is, moreover, one notable though very early
attempt by Maitland to see his own contemporary political
concerns in the context of the history of English political
thought, written long before he had read Gierke, and even before
he had become a lawyer, much less a legal historian. It is the
dissertation he wrote, unsuccessfully, for a Fellowship at Trinity,
Cambridge, in 1875, when he had just taken the recently
established Moral Sciences Tripos, chiefly under the guidance
of Henry Sidgwick. Its title, 'A Historical Sketch of Liberty and
Equality in English Political Philosophy from the time of Hobbes
to the time of Coleridge'—whose scope shows that the history
of political theory was a subject on which virtually no work had
been done—scarcely hid a very topical concern, and it seems to
be derived, above all, from Mill. Democracy, the tyranny of
the majority, the endangered rights of minorities are its
preoccupations, and the tone of the young liberal seems anxious
rather than confident. The contractarian tradition, as the
philosophical grounding for a theory of rights with which to
oppose tyranny, is considered, and found wanting. Maitland
then turns to Coleridge's *On The Constitution of Church and
State* for an alternative: the theory of a constitution embodying
a balanced representation of interests; but he finds Coleridge's
division of them into agricultural and commercial too
mechanical and limited. Lines of class-division cut across
Coleridge's 'interests', but this provides no solution, for,
Maitland says, 'surely it is bad to insist on the discord of class
interests' as the basis for representation.[18] The essay ends with

[18] 'An Historical Sketch of Liberty and Equality as Ideas of English Political

Maitland recommending neither natural rights nor Coleridge's theory of a balance between the two great interests, but the plan of representation which Mill had recommended in *Representative Government*. It is striking how the questions which preoccupied Maitland in his maturity, though not the answers, are anticipated here: the sense that a society composed simply of individuals is helpless against the power of the state, and also that such a conception of society is unrealistic. Hence there is a search for a theory of group interests, and, though Maitland does not arrive at one here, he has already learnt that we need to speak flexibly, to see the individual participating in more than one, and more than one type of, group.

As a historical account of English political thought Maitland's survey is striking, though not, given its period, surprising, in its narrowness. It treats eighteenth-century English political thought in ways not very different from those we saw earlier in Stephen. Hume, for example, is considered chiefly as the destroyer of the theory of the social contract and a founder of utilitarianism. Burke is given some approving words, but, again, is considered essentially in the same terms, as an irresolute critic of contract theory and an imperfect utilitarian. The story Maitland tells, in fact, is centrally one about the rise of utilitarianism, which is then criticized for being simplistic and unhistorical. Nor, it seems, is this selectivity simply the result of Maitland's choice of theme, because he explicitly laments the narrowness which is its consequence: 'The love of simplicity has done vast harm to English political philosophy.'[19] His account of the significance of Mill's *On Liberty* hardly suggests that Maitland was, at this early point at least, like Acton, steeped in the intellectual history of Whiggism: 'The great difference between Mill's *Essay On Liberty* and earlier writings on the same subject is, that Mill resists the presumption that uniformity of action is desirable.' In doing so, and exalting variety, 'Mill broke away from the

Philosophy, from the Time of Hobbes to the Time of Coleridge' (1875), repr. in F W Maitland, *Collected Papers*, ed. H. A. L. Fisher, 3 vols. (Cambridge University Press, 1911), I. 138-9

[19] Ibid. 133.

eighteenth-century tradition.'[20] The importance that Maitland gives to Coleridge's theory of the representation of interests suggests the same obliviousness to a great deal in 'the eighteenth-century tradition' one might have expected him to find sympathetic. By Burkian standards 'Coleridge's theory' was somewhat inflexible and sociologically unimaginative.

So far, then, our suggestion of any possible intellectual genealogy for Maitland's political thinking apart from utilitarianism and German historical jurisprudence seems to have foundered. But there is another possible line of connection, indirect and apparently largely unconscious. It lies in his reasons for preferring Mill's scheme of representation, in *Representative Government*, to Coleridge's. Interests are more diverse than Coleridge allows for, and Mill's preferred solution takes account of this. But Mill's scheme was, as he himself acknowledged, essentially Thomas Hare's, and when we turn to Hare's work we find that the flexibility and diversity of interests Maitland looked for, and which was to form, in a different and jurisprudential language, the central concern of his mature political writings, is not only the burthen of Hare's work but is directly and in numerous places specifically attributed by him to Burke. 'The spirit of association', the leitmotiv of Maitland's later writings, is Hare's watchword also; his book is a celebration of 'the power of voluntary association' Whether or not Maitland read Hare rather than simply taking his ideas, as he seems to do, essentially through Mill, we can at least allow ourselves to register the continuity of preoccupations when we read in Hare that 'Nothing is more remarkable in the early history of this country, than the disposition to form guilds and associations.'[21] We are reminded of Maitland, too, when Hare writes of 'this voluntary and natural disposition to associate, to which full scope should be given in forming our electoral divisions. It is thus, that, when we amend, we build in the old style.'[22] Here it is hard not to see a bridge being built between Burke and Maitland. The first sentence, up to 'given', could pass as Maitland's with any

---

[20] 'Historical Sketch', in *Collected Papers*, I. 111.
[21] Thomas Hare, *A Treatise on the Election of Representatives* (London, 1859), 38, 53. [22] Ibid. 55.

student of his writings. The second, one of Hare's numerous and explicit echoings of Burke ('the authority so often cited in these pages',[23] as he rightly calls him) could never, in its pious traditionalism, have been by Maitland; his own equivalent acknowledgement would later have been to Gierke. But the fact that Maitland lacked a Whig historian's distinctive kind of reverence for the English past does not make Hare's intermediary position any less noteworthy, nor does the fact that Maitland was apparently unaware of how much lies behind the 'new' theory of representation he at that point admired. He, of all people, would not have neglected, had he been at all vividly conscious of it, the chance to acknowledge a debt to Burke and Hare.

In a sense, in the narrower sphere of electoral reform, Hare was attempting much what Maitland's mature political writings can also be seen as doing: to adapt long-established English notions of corporate rights to the conditions of a modern society Hare's electoral scheme was an attempt to recognize and embody in the electoral system, avowedly in the spirit of Burke, the existence of a multiplicity of congeries of interests and opinions. Hare was making the justified point that in a fluid, mobile, and individualistic society—though these were not quite his terms—the traditional territorial basis for the franchise, taking a town or geographical area as the constituency to be represented, was no longer appropriate. Substantial bodies of common interest and opinion went unrepresented if they were geographically widely spread. His remedy was their incorporation as electorates.

Maitland's later writings transpose this from the organization of the franchise into a lawyer's interest in the process of incorporation generally, but the vision of modern society is similar and so is the nature of the enthusiasm. When Maitland wrote in his Fellowship dissertation that 'Men do not want to vote only in their economic character, they want to vote as Churchmen, as Dissenters, as Total Abstainers, as friends of Peace at any price,'[24] he stated in his drier idiom a central theme of Hare's proposal and unconsciously looked forward

---

[23] Ibid. 56.
[24] 'Historical Sketch', in *Collected Papers*, 1. 140.

to his own continuing interest in the diversity of forms of affiliation and association. And as he seems to have shed the influence of Mill's anxiety and even pessimism over minority rights, which marks his early dissertation, his outlook became in some respects more like Hare's, for Hare too writes like an optimist.

Maitland's career as a social and political theorist, if one counts the 1875 dissertation as part of it, follows a highly unusual trajectory for a Victorian liberal—perhaps unusual for anyone; he seems to become more cheerful. He never lost his hostility to the notion of an absolute sovereign, or his interest in minority rights, but he seems largely to have shed the explicit fear of democracy expressed in the fellowship dissertation. In the introduction to Gierke a quarter of a century later, though he is still hostile to the sovereign state and tender to minority rights, he is optimistic and even sunny What has happened in the meanwhile is that Maitland, as a lawyer and a medievalist, rather than an apprentice political philosopher, has had his attention drawn from politics to society, from classics of political thought to law reports and medieval corporations. He is no longer concerned with the question of representation but he has learnt to put confidence, in other ways, in the spontaneous and diverse energies and associative power of modern society

It is true that an autocratic, bureaucratized form of modern society was possible. It was represented for him, as for so many English liberals, by France. This is a position which recalls not only Tocqueville, whom Maitland certainly did read, but also Burke's attack on the centralizing, rationalizing, levelling character of the French Revolution, and the individualism of the theory of natural rights, by which the commonwealth, as Burke said, is 'disconnected into the dust and powder of individuality' [25] But again the contrast is one between defence and attack. The mature Maitland sees the individualistic political theories of natural rights and of utilitarianism as outmoded. The modern age of the later nineteenth century is

---

[25] Burke, *Reflections*, in *Writings and Speeches*, iii. 358. Maitland used the same metaphor applied to France: 'Moral Personality and Legal Personality', *Collected Papers*, iii. 311.

one of multiple spontaneous organizations, of ready incorporation, of collectivities rather than individuals. Collectivism and collectivity were words of ill-repute for most later nineteenth-century liberals, but Maitland is able to reconcile them with a cheerful liberalism by the crucial use of the plural. An *ancien régime* of status distinction and multiple corporations had indeed been succeeded in the earlier nineteenth century, he implies, by an age of individualism, and that age was now being replaced by a new age of corporateness. So far Maitland's historical story agreed with Dicey's famous one in *Law and Opinion in the Nineteenth Century*; but Maitland has none of Dicey's pessimism, because where in the modern age of collectivism Dicey sees uniformity, Maitland sees multiplicity and energy 'Half a century ago,' he wrote in his 1903 essay 'Moral Personality and Legal Personality',

no longer was there much, if anything, to be said of exceptional classes, of nobles, clerics, monks, serfs, slaves, excommunicants or outlaws. Children there might always be, and lunatics, but women had been freed from tutelage. The march of the progressive societies was, as we all know, from status to contract. And now? And now that forlorn old title [he means legal status] is wont to introduce us to ever new species and new genera of persons, to vivacious controversy, to teeming life; and there are many to tell us that the line of advance is no longer from status to contract, but through contract to something that contract cannot explain, and for which our best, if an inadequate name, is the personality of the organised group.[26]

Six years earlier, in his Ford Lectures, *Township and Borough*, he had told his Oxford audience more succinctly that 'If we look at the doings of our law courts, we may feel inclined to reverse a famous judgement and to say that while the individual is the unit of ancient, the corporation is the unit of modern law '[27] The target in both cases is Henry Maine, and Maitland is taking an impish pleasure in reversing two of Maine's famous epigrammatic dicta—'From Status to Contract' was of course Maine's formula for progress. As we have seen, in his own gloomy perception of a coming age of collectivism, in *Popular Government*, he saw only a

[26] Ibid. 315.
[27] F W Maitland, *Township and Borough* (Cambridge University Press, 1898), 13.

putting of progress, unaccountably and wantonly, into reverse. The gloom was because, like Dicey, Maine saw the consequence as a stagnant uniformity, the result of oppressive control by an interfering and omnicompetent sovereign democratic state, where Maitland saw multiplicity, 'teeming life' As we saw earlier, part of the glum apprehensiveness of mid-nineteenth-century liberals like Mill and Maine was related to their proneness to think in terms of a unitary historical process, with a definite line of direction.[28] It was a belief which made for anxiety because of a tendency to extrapolate: either society was moving in a progressive direction or it was doing the reverse; what had once been the source of the liberal's confidence, belief in a single 'movement of society', was now often a cause for dismay

Maitland rejected the over-ambitiousness of such large-scale historical conceptions. For him, as a practising historian, the tendencies of any age were multiple and the future largely unpredictable. It was a scepticism which brings him closer, in some ways, to eighteenth-century Whig attitudes than to nineteenth-century liberal ones based on a general theory of progress. But if such theories of progress were propounded, Maitland was prepared to take them on, up to a point, at their own game, and to turn them mischievously to paradox, as he here does with Maine. More seriously, he doubted the whole conceptual basis of Maine's historical scheme. Maitland constantly challenged Maine's version of the history of property relations. Maine's scheme suggested that individual ownership of property was gradually—and progressively—disentangled from collective ownership. Maitland disbelieved in an original collective ownership because he saw the theory of corporate identity, on which he assumed it must rest, as a highly sophisticated one.[29] He approached Maine's theory with the tools provided by Gierke's theory of legal personality, which implied a sharp distinction between the *Gesellschaft*,

---

[28] See above, pp. 103, 111.
[29] e.g. 'Archaic Communities', in *Collected Papers*, ii. 337 Cf. *Township and Borough*, p. 12; *Domesday Book and Beyond* (Cambridge University Press, 1907), 341. I have tried to give a fuller account of this point in 'The Village Community and the Uses of History', in N. McKendrick (ed.), *Historical Perspectives: Studies in English Thought and Society in Honour of J. H. Plumb* (London, 1974), 282–4.

partnership, which entailed only joint ownership, and the *Genossenschaft*, a fully corporate body, which, applied to property, meant full collective ownership. Maine would, he correctly implied, have to assume that the *Genossenschaft* was ancient, the *Gesellschaft* modern, because the latter was individualistic, a group of individual shareholders linked by a contract, a deed of partnership. But Maitland, looking at medieval English notions of corporate ownership, in *Township and Borough* and elsewhere, came to the conclusion that the legal concept of corporateness was the modern notion, and in his view a highly valuable one. Hence the inversion of Maine; not 'from status to contract', but something more like the reverse. To Maitland, liberal utilitarianism, which resolved the life of society into the behaviour of individuals, and the Austinian theory of legal sovereignty associated with it, was simply unrealistic: 'our popular English *Staatslehre* if, instead of analysing the contents of a speculative jurist's mind, it seriously grasped the facts of English history, would show some inclination to become a *Korporationslehre* also.'[30]

Maitland enjoyed pointing out the inadequacy of liberal individualism as an account of society, yet he certainly thought of himself as a liberal and it would be an odd definition that denied him the title. But his appeal here to 'the facts of English history' inevitably brings him, unconsciously, close to the pragmatic Whig. Because the latter accepts and hopes to harmonize and perhaps improve what the radical individualist challenges: the intricately corporate, complex, *given* character of English society For the gap between the radical individualist language of the utilitarian or natural rights theorist and 'the facts of English history' was not merely a gap between theory and reality; it was one largely created by the liberal individualist of set polemical purpose: to attack the historically given, multiply corporate, and, as it seemed to the radical, corrupt, as well as inefficient, character of English social life. Individualist political theories, whether of a Paineite or Benthamite kind, were essentially tools of criticism, and their point was the exact opposite of Maitland's; not the celebration

---

[30] Introduction to Otto von Gierke, *Political Theories of the Middle Ages*, trans. with an introd. by F W Maitland (Cambridge University Press, 1900), p. xi.

of corporations and associations but the unmasking of them as 'sinister interests' To Bentham, association was simply another term for conspiracy against the general good: 'A common bond of connection, says Cicero somewhere, has place among all the virtues; to the word *virtue*, substitute the word *abuse* '³¹ The issue between Burkian Whig and Benthamite radical could hardly be more tersely put. Bentham's hostility was metaphysical and linguistic as well as directly political: a society was nothing but the aggregate of individuals who composed it. Utilitarian reductionism—'nothing but'—was both epistemological and socially pointed: as the individual is nothing but the aggregate of his experienced discrete sensations, a society is nothing but an aggregate of individuals. The point is first to make the referents of language concrete, so that the mystifications by which vested interests disguise themselves behind an imposing rhetoric can be dispelled, and the interests themselves brought into a clear light in which their real selfish crudity stands revealed; and second, to reduce the heterogeneous to the commensurable, to resolve the language of 'interests' into identical individual units of pleasurable or painful sensation, and hence to permit the application of a radical cost-benefit analysis to all social institutions. And if we are prepared to concede the practical influence of Benthamite ideas on the reform of English institutions between the 1820s and the 1870s, then we might say that Maitland and his generation were the beneficiaries of that scouring process. So, by 1900, it was possible to celebrate corporateness and the multiplicity of social interests it reflected, not as a conservative defending entrenched vested interests, but as a liberal celebrating the spontaneous associative energy of human beings and the social variety created by it. It was possible too, by the early twentieth century, to see the Anglican Church as Figgis did, not as a collection of indefensible privileges but as a body entitled to the corporate rights of people joined for a common purpose in an enduring association, no less than a jointstock company or a trade union; 'corporation' and 'abuse' were no longer interchangeable terms.

---

³¹ Jeremy Bentham, *The Book of Fallacies* (London, 1824), 365. Emphasis original.

If we ask what, putting aside specific questions of possible intellectual connection, is the relation between Maitland and earlier English defences of forms of corporate life against utilitarian individualism and the power of the sovereign state, it seems that what Maitland did, aided by Gierke's theory of the real personality of groups, was to break the connection, characteristically assumed by both Whigs and Tories, between the idea of corporate rights and the concept of tradition or prescription. Usually, in such defences, it had been essentially *ancient* rights that were in question. The rights of corporate bodies, no less than of individual freeholders, were, in the eighteenth century, so much taken for granted that to speak of a 'theory' of corporate rights would imply a degree of self-consciousness that was scarcely present. The outcome of the Civil War and the Revolution of 1688 had precluded any possibility that the English monarchy might become a rationalizing, centralizing autocracy The habit of thinking in terms of ancient corporate privileges, already deeply entrenched, was reinforced. The Civil War had in a legal sense been fought to settle the respective claims of the estates of the realm: the prerogatives of the Crown and the rights and privileges of Parliament. Among the chief offences, in the eyes of their opponents, of the later Stuarts, and particularly James II, had been the attack on the borough corporations and on the privileges of the Church of England and Magdalen College. It was characteristic, if slightly ironical, that the Wilkes affair in the 1760s, in one sense the beginning of a new, populist kind of politics, should have crucially involved a conflict between the privileges of Parliament and those of the City of London.[32]

This was not to say that incorporation was easy The legacy of the South Sea Bubble was a suspicion of joint-stock enterprises and a disposition to impose unlimited liability which lasted until the legislation of the 1850s.[33] Maitland pointed out, in a classic essay, that in England the legal device of the trust had had to supply the remedy for the difficulty of

---

[32] See J. R. Pole, *Political Representation*, pp. 389–90.
[33] This could be either approved or disapproved of from a *laissez-faire*, individualist point of view. See W L. Burn, *The Age of Equipoise* (London, 1964), 221.

obtaining full corporate personality [34] And of course, after the publication of the *Wealth of Nations*, one kind of corporate existence, the established trading monopoly, was regarded with a hostile eye by advanced economic thinkers.

But ancient privileges were part of the fabric of life and the constitution of liberty The French Revolution, in its Civil Constitution of the Clergy, presented an example at once of centralization and autocratic power, of an attack on property, and of the violation of ancient corporate privilege. Burke's denunciation provided a rhetoric for nineteenth-century opposition, Tory rather than Whig, to modest English measures of rationalization and centralization—the Municipal Corporations Act, the Poor Law, the Ecclesiastical Commission, the establishment of Commissions for various purposes—from the 1830s onward. Hostility to these could sometimes unite opposite ends of the political spectrum, Tories and radical ancient constitutionalists; for both, the rhetoric of inherited—sometimes already deplorably abrogated—rights was readily available. We can see it, for example, in the young Disraeli, in his *Vindication of the English Constitution* (1835), denouncing the Whig government for having, as he put it, declared war on all the great national institutions:

> It is these institutions which make us a nation. Without our Crown, our Church, our Universities, our great municipal and commercial corporations, our Magistracy, and its dependent scheme of provincial polity, the inhabitants of England, instead of being a nation, would present only a mass of individuals governed by a metropolis, whence an arbitrary senate would issue the stern decrees of its harsh and heartless despotism    the whole land a prey to the most degrading equality, the equality that levels not the equality that elevates
> a state of society which France has accomplished, and to which the Whigs are hurrying us    [35]

We see it, too, in the most vehement of all English advocates of local autonomy, Josuah Toulmin Smith, writing just over a decade later. Toulmin Smith was an ancient constitutionalist who saw such measures as the Public Health Act and the new

---

[34] 'Trust and Corporation', in *Collected Papers*, vol. iii.
[35] Disraeli the Younger, *Vindication of the English Constitution in a Letter to a Noble Lord* (London, 1835), 181-2.

Poor Law as gross, despotic invasions of constitutional rights. He presented recent English History as a Manichaean struggle between two rival principles, 'Centralization' and 'Local Self-Government', rather as an eighteenth-century Whig had typically seen it as a conflict between liberty and despotism. He had the Country Whig's fear of the encroachment of despotism (now called 'centralization') by stealth under the outward forms of a free constitution.[36] Antiquarian, autodidact, and polymath, Toulmin Smith was an odd mixture. In many respects he speaks in the fashionable liberal language of the period, of 'centralization', and of public spirit and participation as the guarantee of liberty, antidote to class war, and prophylactic against revolutionary demagoguery [37] He was an early employer of the new term 'bureaucracy' In these respects he sounds like a modish liberal or progressive Whig, for whom France, as always, is the awful warning.

But he was also an antiquarian, recognizably the heir to Country Party and radical ancient constitutionalist obsessions: the adulation of good King Alfred; ancient popular rights; the superiority of Common Law to statute. His preferred authorities are those of an eighteenth-century Country Whig— the Anglo-Saxon laws, Chief Justice Coke, Fletcher of Saltoun. Predictably he denounces standing armies and the National Debt, and favours annual Parliaments.[38] The transposition of Country Party enthusiasms and animosities into the liberal language of the mid-nineteenth century is sometimes quaint,· as when James II is castigated as an opponent of 'Local Self-Government',[39] but it can also be pointed, as when he adapts the old language of patriotism and public spirit to attack the selfishness of liberal individualism,[40] rather as the young liberal authors of *Essays on Reform* were to do in the following decade. The old dichotomy of energetic public virtue set against selfish private leisure and the mere pursuit of commercial profit is still alive here. Toulmin Smith's combination of antiquarian zest and enthusiasm for the traditions of English local

---

[36] Josuah Toulmin Smith, *Local Self-Government and Centralization: The Characteristics of Each; and its Practical Tendencies as Affecting Social, Moral and Political Welfare and Progress* (London, 1851), 29
[37] Ibid. 42–3.   [38] Ibid. 197, 203.   [39] Ibid. 194.
[40] Ibid. 41–2.

self-government was a common one, though in his case it had a populist and in some ways old-fashioned cast. We see it in more sophisticated forms, for example, in the Whig historians, Freeman, Stubbs, and John Richard Green. For them too, English independence and political capacity is rooted in local self-government even more than in Parliament itself; historically given institutional diversity is to be cherished; the consciousness of freedom and the sense of enduring tradition are crucially related.[41]

Of course there are mid-Victorian examples in which the case for local independence is made, often under Tocqueville's influence, more purely politically and sociologically rather than historically; the best-known example would be Mill and one could readily find others. There are also attempts to see other forms of spontaneous social organizations and even expressions of specific sectional interests, besides those of local communities, as valid and calling for recognition. If we go back as far as Burke we can see that in making a case for the recognition of the emergence of new 'interests' and forms of opinion which were not traditional and incorporate but recent and fluid, and which might need Parliamentary representation,[42] he was making a tentative but crucial move from the traditional to the sociological vindication of the rights of various forms of collective life; their claim required recognition not because they were ancient but because they had come to exist. But Burke's attitude to the power of association was also wary, as when in his famous vindication of party affiliations in politics, for example, he had to work hard to distinguish party from faction.[43] Confronted by the French Revolution, he fell back on a distinction between the traditional local bonds of a rural society, 'our habitual provincial connection', which were to be cherished, and the feverishness of urban sociability, 'the municipal clubs, cabals and confederacies' which he saw with acute apprehension and

---

[41] For a fuller account see Stefan Collini, Donald Winch, and John Burrow, *That Noble Science of Politics: A Study in Nineteenth-century Intellectual History* (Cambridge University Press, 1983), 202-3.

[42] On this see Pole, *Political Representation*, pp. 443-4.

[43] 'When bad men combine, the good must associate', etc. 'Thoughts on the Cause of the Present Discontents', in *Writings and Speeches*, I. 526.

in terms of the old vocabulary—'cabals', etc.—traditionally applied in the denunciation of faction.[44]

If we move forward to Mill we find, of course, no similar prejudice in favour of the rural and traditional. His essay on 'Civilisation', for example, written in 1836, gives a virtually unqualified endorsement to spontaneous association of all kinds, including the Comtist or Coleridgian notion of a formal organization for the clerisy which he later came to see as a potential instrument of intellectual despotism.[45] In *Representative Government* Mill follows Hare in arguing that representation need not be based only on the traditional unit of the geographical locality We hear the voice of the *déraciné* in the claims on behalf of 'people who have other feelings and interests which they value more than they do their geographical ones', and that of the metropolitan progressive in the criticism of 'an inveterate spirit of locality'[46] as an obstacle to improvement. But the Benthamite suspicion of 'sinister interests'[47] is still alive too: the various sectional interests must be held in check. The thought and tone are often not very different from the eighteenth-century rhetoric which set private interest against patriotism and virtue, and of course the fostering of 'public spirit' is a central concern for Mill. It is here that forms of association which are essentially aspects of self-*government* are bound to seem superior to all others. Participation in the exercise of public responsibility, at any level, if it be only the jury or the vestry, is a 'school of public spirit', where a man is introduced to 'elevated considerations' and has 'to weigh interests not his own'[48] 'Virtue' and 'interest' are continuing to play out their long dialectic.

Of course, we are in danger of exaggerating; the distinction between public and sectional was not easily or sharply drawn. The Christian Socialists of the 1840s and 1850s, for example, like the Comtists, extolled co-operation rather than individual competition as the basis of economic life. In this spirit, trade

---

[44] *Reflections*, ibid. iii. 521.
[45] 'Civilization', *London and Westminster Review* (1836), repr. in *Mill's Essays on Literature and Society*, ed. J. B. Schneewind (London, 1965), 170–2. Cf. his review of Guizot (1845) in *Collected Works*, xx. 270.
[46] *Representative Government*, pp. 461, 417
[47] Mill recognizes its Benthamite origin, ibid. 441. [48] Ibid. 412.

unions, despite their sectional character, could be hailed as nurseries of co-operation and schools of education in public life for the working classes.[49] Yet in all of this it would be perhaps an exaggeration to speak of a theory of voluntary associations, and in so far as there was one, it was, as much as anything, a theory of moral education; the tone was relentlessly high. Maitland, by comparison, propounds a theory of associations and a view of the fecundity of corporate life which is at once more technical and more promiscuous, as well as less immediately political. It made a difference that Maitland was a disciple of Gierke rather than, like so many Victorian liberals, of Tocqueville; the medieval *Genossenschaft* rather than the New England town-meeting or, for that matter, the early English folk-moot was his model, and he was a leading critic of attempts to link the origins of English local government to the ancient Teutonic village community His greatest interest was in spontaneously created elements of social life which could not be construed as he put it, 'as a piece of the State's mechanism' [50] He transposed the veneration with which historians like Stubbs, Freeman, and Green had regarded small self-governing social units, considered as the building-blocks of English constitutional liberty, to the fluid conditions of a commercial and industrial society [51] Though an agnostic with a general taste for deflation, he sometimes writes of the vitality and diversity of forms of collective life with an enthusiasm which makes him seem, if not Burkian, at any rate *anima naturaliter Burkiana*. Yet he can also sound as anti-traditionalist as Mill. He was, as befitted a pupil of Sidgwick, a utilitarian in his appraisals, through one who had repudiated utilitarian individualism as an analysis of modern society Though a medievalist, he had a coolness towards appeals to ancient rights and traditional practices akin to that of a Humean sceptical Whig.[52]

---

[49] e.g. R. H. Hutton, 'The Political Character of the Working Classes', in *Essays on Reform* (London, 1867).

[50] Gierke, *Political Theories*, Introd., pp. xxi, xxiv

[51] Burrow, 'The Village Community', in N. McKendrick (ed.), *Historical Perspectives*, pp. 278–81.

[52] e.g. 'The Law of Real Property' (1879), *Collected Papers*, i. 195. 'The German Legal Code' (1906), ibid. iii. 476 ff.

It was the refusal of Maitland's theory of corporate rights to take sides, even by rhetorical implication, between different *kinds* of association, traditional or otherwise, that made the ideas he largely inspired seem, in the years after 1900, in the broadest sense liberal rather than conservative; welcoming to diversity, opposed only to a state-imposed uniformity and bureaucracy It was a way of thinking that seemed to transcend class; available alike to capitalists and trade-unionists, conservatives, churchmen, and Guild Socialists. But this catholicity carried a price. I have argued that Maitland's thinking can plausibly be placed (though its immediate sources in important respects lay elsewhere) in a Whig tradition endorsing a multiplicity of social energies. Yet there is a crucial difference. Those energies are now characteristically seen not as represented in the sovereign parliament as well as in society, but as set against it. Hence the problem arises, as it did not in quite the same way for a Whig theory of a mixed or composite government, whether they are ultimately subject to the sovereign central authority or in some ways elude it.

There was a sense in which the argument was strongest, as in Maitland's case, when it was addressed to the question of the conditions of legal corporateness. But as the argument became more broadly political, pluralists ran at once into the problem they were never able to solve: what to do about the sovereign State? Either the subsidiary forms of social organization were properly to be seen as independent or they were not. If they were, how many of them should be recognized, how were the relations between them to be regulated, and how were conflicts between them and the central authority to be resolved? If they were not independent—and it was never seriously argued that they should be beyond the reach of the law—then their qualified autonomy was merely a concession which Parliament might or might not choose to allow In the absence of a written constitution and judicial review, such issues were unsolvable. Ultimately, pluralist arguments, to acquire real purchase, needed to address the question of the constitution itself, as in proposals for an 'Industrial Parliament' of 'producers', alongside the ancient territorial one.[53]

---

[53] e.g. Sydney and Beatrice Webb, *A Constitution for the Socialist Commonwealth of Great Britain* (London, 1920).

Such industrial corporatism, in various forms, attracted attention in the 1920s and 1930s, but it remained to be shown how it could be made compatible with the central power of the state, on any terms more realistic than the sham—a discouraging precedent for liberals—of the Fascist Corporate State.

As a matter of intellectual fashion too, pluralist arguments of this kind became outmoded. Most obviously, in political and philosophical terms, what Maitland's German-accented theory of the corporation was doing was offering a parallel to the current philosophical idiom for talking about the State. The metaphysical theory of the real personality of groups was the pluralist counter to the—also German-inspired— metaphysical theory of the State. The period around 1900 was one when it became more fashionable than ever before in England to speak of the State in Hegelian Idealist terms as the organized real will of society The classic case is Bernard Bosanquet's *Philosophical Theory of the State* (1899).

What Maitland, employing the same organicist Germanic terminology, was doing was to point out that, if we are to talk of the collective will of groups considered as metaphysical persons, there are many more such group persons than simply the State—in this way turning a collectivist idiom into a liberal or Whiggish one. As he says, 'a doctrine which makes some way in England, ascribes to the state, or more vaguely, the Community, not only a real will, but even "the" real will, and it must occur to us to ask whether what is thus affirmed in the case of the State can be denied in the case of other organised groups' [54]

But this metaphysical idiom for political theory declined over the next few years, as Idealist metaphysics in general fell victim to the change in philosophical fashion back towards empiricism, beginning before 1914 in the work of Russell and Moore. A political position based on a metaphysical theory of the real personality of groups, and systematically conflating description and prescription in its rejection of individualism and the concept of sovereignty, was expressed in what, by the 1940s and 1950s was an outmoded

[54] Gierke, *Political Theories*, p. xi.

philosophical idiom.⁵⁵ Its declining repute was in that sense an aspect of the general philosophical disrespect for much which had traditionally passed as political theory, leading in 1956 to the now famous declaration that political philosophy was dead.⁵⁶

That claim is now regarded as excessive, yet it still seems appropriate to bring the Whig-Liberal lines of thought we have been considering here to an end with an episode which lost impetus, as well as, sometimes, any recognizable connection with liberalism, in the 1930s. In so far as liberal political theory shows vitality today (sometimes, confusingly, under the label of 'conservative') it does so most recognizably in the tradition of liberal-individualist theories of rights, or of economic *laissez-faire*, which I have deliberately set aside here.

It would be possible, of course, to carry further some of the themes I have considered. Some pundits of the inter-war period—Ernest Barker, A. D Lindsay, for example—were bearers of important continuities;⁵⁷ Barker roundly declared that he belonged to 'the ancient Whig tradition' ⁵⁸ It is unlikely, to say the least, that the conflicts of central with local authorities, the qualified autonomy of trade unions and other corporate bodies, the issues of federalism, devolution, and the franchise will attract no more reflection and theoretical discussion. But for the moment, at least, the simple, dualistic division of political theories into individualist and collectivist or socialist, which established itself in Britain a century ago, remains, for all its crudity, the most obvious way of describing their outstanding differences. It is because this is predominantly the way we talk now that we are sometimes tempted to assume that these are also the categories through which we should try to understand the political thought of the past. These lectures have been intended as a modest protest against that assumption.

---

⁵⁵ e.g. David P Derham, 'Theories of Legal Personality', in L. C. Webb, *Legal Personality and Political Pluralism* (Melbourne, 1958), 1-2.

⁵⁶ Peter Laslett (ed.), *Philosophy, Politics, and Society* (Oxford, 1956), editor's introd., p. vii.

⁵⁷ On such continuities generally, as part of the culture of the educated class in the early 20th cent., see Collini in Collini, Winch, and Burrow, *That Noble Science*, pp. 375-6; on Barker and Lindsay, Julia Stapleton, 'Academic Political Thought and the Development of Political Studies in Britain, 1900-1950', unpub. D. Phil. thesis, University of Sussex (1986), esp. ch. 4.

⁵⁸ Ibid. 80. I am grateful to Dr Stapleton for permission to cite her work.

# Index

Acton, John Emerich Dalberg 1, 14, 35, 136, 137
  his pluralism 131–5
Addison, Joseph 3
Alfred, King 147
American democracy 44–6, 79
Aquinas, Thomas 1, 133
Aristotle 28, 116
Arnold, Matthew 31, 76, 83, 95
Arnold, Thomas 18, 48
Asiatic despotism 87 n., 88, 116
  effeminacy 87, 88
  servitude 86
Austinian theory of sovereignty 143

Bacon, Francis 19
Bagehot, Walter viii, 107, 113, 120, 123 n.
  conception of progress 70, 72, 78, 108–10
  constitutional views 12, 112, 128
  on public opinion 67–70, 72, 73, 74, 75, 76 n.
Balzac, Honoré de 99
Barker, Ernest 130, 153
Bentham, Jeremy 2, 3, 9, 17, 18, 38, 70, 78 n., 144,
  also Benthamism, Benthamite 6, 37–8, 48, 125, 143, 149
Bismarck, Otto von 133
Blackstone, William 31 n., 55, 114
Bolingbroke, Henry St John, Viscount 8, 27
Bosanquet, Bernard 99, 152
Brodrick, George 23, 46 n., 71 n.
Brooke, Rupert 97

Bryce, James 14, 45 n., 46 n., 47 n., 48, 127
Burke, Edmund viii, x, 3, 7, 9, 10, 14, 15, 17, 73, 82, 102, 106, 112, 125 n., 126, 128, 131, 134, 135, 137, 138, 139, 140, 146, 148, 150
  on polity and society 34–6
  on prejudice 53, 56, 57, 60, 61, 62, 63, 64–7
  on representation of interests 118–20
Burne-Jones, Edward 97
Butler, Joseph 10
Butler, Lady 96
Byron, George Gordon, Lord:
  J. S. Mill on 78–9, 101

Carlyle, A. J. vii, 1
Carlyle, Thomas 59, 77, 80
  also Carlylean 81, 87, 88 n.
'Chinese stationariness' 107, 117, 120–1, 124
Christian Socialism 46, 149
Cicero 144
civic humanism 27, 36, 42, 43, 47, 92, 102
  see also Country Party and Machiavellian
civil society 20
  history of 26, 27, 32
Clough, Arthur Hugh 82 n.
Cobbett, William 59
Coke, Chief Justice 147
Cole, G. D H. 131
Coleridge, S. T (also Coleridgian) 18, 59, 77, 80, 81, 101, 136, 137, 138, 149

# 156　　　　　Index

Collini, Stefan 83, 96
commercial society 30, 37, 80, 91
Comte, August (also Comtism, Comtist) 15, 46, 48, 73, 94, 101, 149
Condorcet, F M. de 58, 59, 61, 73
Constant, Benjamin 28
Coulthard, Joseph 82
Country Party 11, 17, 27
　see also civic humanism, Harringtonian 34, 42, 54, 55, 80, 81, 85, 90, 91, 92, 102, 105, 106, 107, 117, 118, 128, 147

Darwin, Charles 108
Darwinism 108, 109
　see also Social Darwinism
Dicey, A. V 48, 127, 128, 129, 141, 142
Disraeli, Benjamin 146

Ecclesiastical Commission 146
*Edinburgh Review* 11, 31 n., 38, 39, 66, 67, 102
Edinburgh Reviewers 12, 40, 42-4, 73, 106
*Essays on Reform* 10, 23, 45 n., 46-8, 127, 128, 147, 150 n.

Fabians 129
Factory Acts 59
Fascist Corporate State 152
federalism 132, 134, 135
Ferguson, Adam 9, 77, 80, 92
Figgis, John Neville 1, 14, 131, 135, 144
Fletcher of Saltoun 25 n., 147
Forbes, Duncan 28, 31 n., 56
Forster, E. M. 98 n.
Fox, Charles James 42
Free Church of Scotland 131
Freeman, Edward 1, 14, 123, 132, 133, 134, 148, 150
French Revolution 29, 33, 35-7, 40, 41, 63-4, 65, 133-4, 146

Garibaldi, Giuseppe 47
George, Henry 129
Gibbon, Edward 33, 51, 57-8, 60, 65, 85, 87, 88, 98, 99, 117, 121-2, 123, 126 n., 132, 134
Gierke, Otto von 135, 136, 139, 140, 142, 145, 150
Gladstone, W E. 21, 46, 74 n.
Godwin, Earl of Wessex 1
Godwin, William 57, 60, 61
Goethe, J. W von 77, 82, 94, 95, 101
Gordon, General Charles 96
Gordon, Thomas 116
Grattan, Henry 13
Green, John Richard 148, 150
Green, T H. 18, 48 n.
Grey, Henry George, 3rd Earl 128
Guild Socialism 131, 151
Guizot, François 108, 122-3, 132, 134

Hallam, Henry 68
Halévy, Elie 18
Hare, Thomas 17, 123, 138-9, 149
Harrington, James 88, 114
Harringtonian republicanism 25, 89-90, 118
Hegel, G. W F 6 n., 152
Helvétius, Claude Adrien 58
Hobbes, Thomas 3, 19, 114, 136
Hobbesian conception of man 4-5
Hobhouse, L. T 82, 99, 128
Hobson, J. A. 128
Holbach, Paul Henri 58
Holland, Henry Vassall, Lord 11
Holland House 11, 67
Houghton, Lord (Richard Monckton Milnes) 48 n.
Humboldt, Wilhelm von viii, 16, 81, 82, 84, 93-5, 99, 101
Hume, David x, 3, 5, 8, 10, 12 n. 20, 28, 29, 30, 33, 34, 35, 40, 42, 66, 67, 68, 69, 70, 117, 120-1, 122, 137

# Index

on political irrationality 51-6
on superstition and enthusiasm
    64-5
Hutton, R. H.  47 n., 68 n., 150 n.
Huxley, T H.  22

Idealism, metaphysical 6, 18,
    101, 152
Idea of the State 99, 152
individualism 2-5, 18, 104,
    110-11, 112, 125, 129,
    142-5, 147
individuality 81-5, 97, 104,
    111-12, 127, 129

Jackson, Andrew 44
Jacobins 35, 57, 92, 128
James II 145, 147
Jeffrey, Francis x, 12, 38, 39,
    42-4, 53, 66, 85, 112
Johnson, Samuel 1

Kingsley, Charles 87
Kipling, Rudyard 96, 97-9
*Kulturkampf* 133

*laissez-faire* 3, 4, 12, 30
Laski, Harold 131
Lawrence, T E.  97
Lecky, W E. H. 13, 14, 127, 128
Liberal Unionists 129
Liberalism/Liberals, New 18,
    128, 129, 131
Liberals, University 10, 18
Liberty and Property Defence
    League 129
Lindsay, A. D 133
Livy 29
Locke, John (also Lockian) 3, 6,
    8, 26, 37, 46
Lowe, Robert 21, 44 n., 46, 111

Macaulay, Thomas Babington 1,
    16, 20, 28, 29, 30, 31, 33,
    34, 38, 53, 54, 76 n., 91, 92
on the constitution 102-3,
    105, 128
on James Mill 15, 19, 41

on political irrationality 67-8,
    74
relation to the eighteenth
    century 11-13
Machiavelli, Niccolo 17, 114,
    115
Machiavellian republicanism 11,
    17, 88-9, 91, 92, 93, 95
Mackintosh, James x, 12, 45, 57,
    61-2, 64, 112
Maine, Henry 13, 14, 22, 78,
    107, 108-9, 120, 129, 141,
    142, 143
Maistre, Joseph de 4 n.
Maitland, Frederick William viii,
    ix, 131, 152
corporatist ideas of 135-45,
    150-1
Malthus, Thomas Robert 59
Mandeville, Bernard de 52, 53
Marx, Karl 6 n., 22
also Marxists 129
Maurice, Frederick Denison 77, 101
Mazzini, Giuseppe 46, 47, 48
Mill, James 3, 4, 15, 19, 24, 38,
    40, 41, 75, 91, 99, 105, 128
Mill, John Stuart viii, 3, 15, 16,
    17, 20, 22, 24-7, 45 n., 54,
    66, 71, 72, 73, 74, 75, 76,
    117, 120, 123, 127, 132,
    134, 135, 136, 137, 138,
    140, 148, 149, 150
comparisons with contemporaries
    107-8, 110-13
on civilization 77-81
on democracy 103-4
on individuality 82-6, 92-5
*On Representative
    Government* 104-7
Millar, John 9, 15, 61, 62-3,
    78, 92
Molesworth, Robert 29
Molyneaux, William 29
Montesquieu, Charles de
    Secondat 17, 28, 86 n., 115,
    116, 117
Moore, G. E. 152
Morley, John 14, 22, 73-5

Moyle, Walter 114, 115
Municipal Corporations Act 146

Namier, Sir Lewis 17
natural rights 46, 62, 125, 143
Nerval, Gérard de 79
Neville, Henry 25 n.
New Liberalism, *see* Liberalism, New
Newbolt, Sir Henry 96, 97
Nietzsche, Friedrich 77, 97, 99

Osborne judgment 131

Paine, Thomas (also Paineite) 57, 61, 64, 128, 143
Paley, William (also Paleyan) 54–7, 60, 74, 112
Pater, Walter 95, 97
Pearson, C. H. 99, 127
Philosophic Radicalism, Philosophic Radicals 10, 18, 19, 38, 40, 59, 73, 128
Plutarch 29
Pocock, J. G. A. 36–7, 88, 91
Political Economy 3, 6, 19, 26, 60, 124
Political Pluralism 130 and ch. 6 *passim*
Polybius, Polybian 28, 106, 110, 113, 114
Poor Law 59
Price, Cormell 97
Price, Richard 128

Reid, Thomas 39
Ricardo, David 3
Rothblatt, Sheldon 83
Rousseau, Jean Jacques (and Rousseauist) 29, 77, 93, 111, 126, 134
Russell, Bertrand 152
Russell, Lord John 12
Rutson, A. O 45 n., 47 n.

Saint Simon, Henri de 108; Saint Simonians 24, 77, 81
Schiller, Friedrich 93 n.

Scott, Robert Falcon 96
Scottish Enlightenment 11, 17, 26, 30, 42, 43, 79, 90, 91, 92, 102, 108, 128
Seeley, J. R. 132
Shaftesbury, 3rd Earl of 10, 12
Shaw, George Bernard 127
Sidgwick, Henry 136, 150
'sinister interests' 144, 149
Smiles, Samuel 31, 84
Smith, Adam x, 3, 4, 6, 12, 20, 30, 32, 34, 50, 51, 58, 59, 66, 67, 70, 74, 90–1, 92, 129
Smith, Sydney 76
Social Darwinism 18, 99, 125
Sorel, Georges 77
Southey, Robert 59
South Sea Bubble 145
Spencer, Herbert viii, 3, 4, 72, 78, 129
Stephen, Leslie 8–13, 14, 16, 17, 19, 23, 24, 45 n., 87, 127, 137
Sterling, John 92
Stewart, Dugald 15, 41 n., 43, 53
Stubbs, William 148, 150
Suarez, Francisco 133

Taff Vale judgment 131
Thackeray, William Makepeace 87
Tocqueville, Alexis de (also Tocquevillian) 19, 21, 45, 46, 54, 77, 78, 93, 103, 106, 108, 111, 123, 124, 132, 140, 148, 150
Toulmin Smith, Josuah 146–7
Trenchard, John 25, 27, 41, 114, 116
Turgot, Robert Jacques 73

Utilitarian, Utilitarianism, Utilitarians 3, 5, 12, 19, 39, 125

*virtù*, virtue (civic) 86–9, 91, 92, 99, 149

Wallas, Graham 74

Webb, Sydney and Beatrice 151 n.
Wells, H. G. 127
Whiggism, varieties of 7, 31 n.
Wilkes, John (also Wilkite) 33, 145

Winckelmann, Johann Joachim 95
Wolin, Sheldon 4
Wollstonecraft, Mary 57, 63, 64
Wordsworth, William 78, 101

CPSIA information can be obtained at www.ICGtesting.com
Printed in the USA
BVOW08*1414160816

459165BV00004B/5/P